"This book is biblically grounded and Christ-centered, full of grace and truth. Every chapter raises the bar of Christian living without falling into legalism. One of the most timely and much-needed books I've read in years. I highly recommend it."

> RANDY ALCORN, author, *Heaven* and *The Grace and Truth Paradox*

"Expertly addresses the issues that prompt that subtle, insidious, silent slide away from God that each of us is prone to take. Pay attention to this thought-provoking work and protect your heart for God."

> JAMES MACDONALD, Pastor, Harvest Bible Chapel; teacher, *Walk in the Word*

"This book is biblical, practical, pastoral, and wise. It is honest about the authors' own temptations, and it is so specific it will be controversial! But such a book is greatly needed as a challenge today—for all of us."

> WAYNE GRUDEM, Research Professor of Bible and Theology, Phoenix Seminary

"The strength of the work is that the authors try very hard not to let you forget the sheer God-centeredness of the gospel."

> D. A. CARSON, Research Professor of New Testament, Trinity Evangelical Divinity School

"These skillful soul surgeons are brilliant at diagnosis and treatment, and they will help you see yourself, your sin, and your Savior. I now know the first book I am going to reach for when a Christian is wrestling with worldliness—or isn't but should be! This is a book I will make use of, by God's grace, again and again."

> LIGON DUNCAN, Senior Minister, First Presbyterian Church, Jackson, Mississippi; President, Alliance of Confessing Evangelicals

"Praise God for this little tool—specific enough to be helpful, grace-filled enough to be really helpful!"

> MARK DEVER, Senior Pastor, Capitol Hill Baptist Church; Executive Director, 9Marks Ministries

Worldliness

Crossway books by C. J. Mahaney

Preaching the Cross (coauthor)

*Sex, Romance, and the Glory of God:
What Every Christian Husband Needs to Know*

Worldliness

Resisting the Seduction of a Fallen World

C. J. Mahaney, **Editor**

Craig Cabaniss

Bob Kauflin

Dave Harvey

Jeff Purswell

Foreword by John Piper

CROSSWAY BOOKS

WHEATON, ILLINOIS

Worldliness: Resisting the Seduction of a Fallen World

Copyright © 2008 by Sovereign Grace Ministries

Published by Crossway Books
a publishing ministry of Good News Publishers
1300 Crescent Street
Wheaton, Illinois 60187

Cover design: Matthew Wahl

Cover photograph: Matthew Wahl

First printing 2008

Printed in the United States of America

PDF ISBN: 978-1-4335-0486-0

Mobipocket ISBN: 978-1-4335-0487-7

Library of Congress Cataloging-in-Publication Data
Worldliness : resisting the seduction of a fallen / C.J. Mahaney,
editor ; foreword by John Piper.
    p. cm.
  ISBN 978-1-4335-0280-4 (hc)
    1. Christian life. 2. Worldliness. I.Mahaney, C.J. II. Title.
BV4501.3.W67   2008
241—dc22   2008011647

| LB | | 16 | 15 | 14 | 13 | 12 | 11 | 10 | 09 |
| 14 | 13 | 12 | 11 | 10 | 9 | 8 | 7 | 6 | 5 | 4 |

To the pastors of Sovereign Grace Ministries
with gratitude and respect
for your faithful proclamation of Christ and him crucified

"Far be it from me to boast
except in the cross of our Lord Jesus Christ,
by which the world has been crucified to me,
and I to the world."
Galatians 6:14

Contents

Contributors

Craig Cabaniss planted Grace Church in Frisco, Texas, in 2005 and serves as its senior pastor. He was previously senior pastor of Grace Church in San Diego, California, for nine years.

Dave Harvey serves on the leadership team of Sovereign Grace Ministries, where he oversees church planting and church care. He is the author of *When Sinners Say "I Do": Discovering the Power of the Gospel for Marriage.*

Bob Kauflin is director of worship development for Sovereign Grace Ministries and serves as a pastor and worship leader at Covenant Life Church in Gaithersburg, Maryland. He is the author of *Worship Matters: Leading Others to Encounter the Greatness of God.*

C. J. Mahaney leads Sovereign Grace Ministries in its mission to establish and strengthen local churches. He served as pastor of Covenant Life Church in Gaithersburg, Maryland, for twenty-seven years. His books include *Living the Cross Centered Life.*

Jeff Purswell is dean of the Pastors College of Sovereign Grace Ministries and is a pastor at Covenant Life Church in Gaithersburg, Maryland. He is the editor of *Bible Doctrine*, an abridgment of Wayne Grudem's *Systematic Theology.*

Foreword

BELIEVE IT OR NOT, Noël and I didn't kiss in our wedding. It was the sixties. You had to rebel. You could either take your clothes off, or not kiss. We chose not to kiss. Within the framework of our immaturity, it was a good choice.

That's the way my rebellious streak worked most of the time—in-your-face conservatism. So there, all you copycat worldlings! I'm not gettin' on your liberal wagon.

It's been a useful bent. There's nothing especially godly about it, but it was redeemable. And I pray that over time it has been redeemed. It's truths like those in this book that have made all the difference.

Gospel truths. The gospel makes all the difference between whether you are merely conservative or whether you are conquering worldliness in the power of the Spirit for the glory of Christ.

C. J. Mahaney and his gang, as always, are in the business of applying the gospel. What does it look like when the blood of Christ governs the television and the Internet and the iPod and the checkbook and the neckline? Most people have never even asked this question, let alone answered it. The only way most folks know how to draw lines is with rulers. The idea that lines might come into being freely and lovingly (and firmly) as the fruit of the gospel is rare. That's why this book is valuable.

11

This band of gospel-lovers is also in touch with the real challenges that we face in music and movies and media and material possessions and modesty. They are writing as fellow strugglers in the world. They are not writing as culture-fleers or culture-deniers. They are pleading for discernment, and they are persuaded that movie ratings do not equal biblical discernment.

They are eager for the church to "Enjoy the world . . . Engage the world . . . Evangelize the world." But they know that we will never be useful to the world if we are being deeply shaped by the world. And we *will* be shaped by the world without intentional efforts not to be.

Read this book sympathetically. That is, when you see the sentence, "The world God forbids us to love is the fallen world," don't say, "Hey, God loved the world! It says so in John 3:16!" These guys aren't stupid. In fact, they are smart. So read on, and see what the context demands. Be smart with them.

A word to pastors: this book is a gift to you. It will help you help others—by the modeling that's done here and by the exegetical reflection and by the biblical and cultural insights. I can see whole churches reading this together as the pastor fleshes out the biblical foundations from the pulpit. What a powerful season that would be in the life of the church.

The apostle Paul has a vision for our minds: "Whatever is true, whatever is honorable, whatever is just, whatever is pure, whatever is lovely, whatever is commendable, if there is any excellence, if there is anything worthy of praise, think about these things" (Phil. 4:8).

May the Lord of all beauty purify our minds so that these are our greatest delights. In the end, the sum of all beauty is Christ, and the sin of all worldliness is to diminish our capacity to see him and be satisfied in him and show him compellingly to a perishing world.

John Piper
Pastor for Preaching and Vision,
Bethlehem Baptist Church
Minneapolis, Minnesota

Chapter One

Is This Verse in Your Bible?

C. J. Mahaney

HUNCHED OVER HIS DESK, penknife in hand, Thomas Jefferson sliced carefully at the pages of Holy Scripture, excising select passages and pasting them together to create a Bible more to his liking. The "Jefferson Bible." A book he could feel comfortable with.

What didn't make it into the Jefferson Bible was anything that conflicted with his personal worldview. Hell? It can't be. The supernatural? Not even worth considering. God's wrath against sin? I don't think so. The very words of God regarded as leftover scraps.

Christians rightly shudder at such arrogant presumption. And no true Christian would be so bold as to attempt to create his or her own Bible, blatantly omitting whatever they don't prefer.

But if we are honest, we too may have to admit that we have a Bible of our own making—a metaphorical one, perhaps, but a cut-and-paste job just the same. For if we ignore any portion of God's Word—whether unintentionally, conveniently, or deliberately—we too are guilty of Jefferson's offense.

Sadly, I've been guilty on more than one occasion. I've opened my Bible and moved quickly to the encouraging and assuring passages, trying to avoid the difficult and challenging passages along the way.

Here's one verse I find easy to ignore. It's the simple, provocative words in 1 John 2:15:

"Do not love the world or anything in the world" (NIV).

There's nothing subtle about this sentence. It's abrupt and to the point—only ten words. It is categorical: "Do *not* love the world." It's comprehensive: "Do not love *anything* in the world." And it's intrusive, strategically aimed at whatever we desire most: "*anything in the world.*"

It forbids worldliness in no uncertain terms.

First John 2:15 isn't a verse we tend to underline when we come across it in our daily Bible reading. We're not inclined to put "Do not love the world" on an index card and rehearse it during our daily commute. We don't hear many sermons on this verse and its prohibition of the sin of worldliness.

We read, we live, as if it doesn't belong in our Bible.

Clip. Clip. Clip.

Before we know it, we have a Bible like Jefferson's, and 1 John 2:15 is nowhere to be found.

Put Away the Scissors

Why do we try to create a Bible exclusive of this command?

Maybe, for all its simplicity, we're not exactly sure what it means. What is the author, John, getting at here? What does it mean for a Christian—what does it mean for *me*—not to love the world?

Does it mean I can't watch MTV or go to an R-rated movie? Do I have to give up my favorite TV shows? Is it okay to watch a movie as long as I fast-forward the sex scene? How much violence or language is too much?

Are certain styles of music more worldly than others? Is the rap or indie music that I'm loading onto my iPod okay?

How do I know if I'm spending too much time playing games or watching YouTube clips online?

Can a Christian try to make lots of money, own a second home, drive a nice car, and enjoy the luxuries of modern life?

Am I worldly if I read fashion magazines and wear trendy clothes? Do I have to be out of style in order to be godly? How short is too short? How low is too low?

How do I know if I'm guilty of the sin of worldliness?

You may have questions like these. But maybe, if you're honest, you don't really want the answers—at least, not from middle-aged pastors like my coauthors and me. You may assume that we're out-of-touch and that worldliness is the predictable concern of men over forty who can't relate to the younger generation.

Maybe you worry that the aim of this book is to impose legalistic restrictions and enforce unrealistic rules. The idea of "resisting the seduction of a fallen world" sounds like something out of an Amish handbook. "Besides," you wonder, "how can we evangelize the world if we don't relate to it?"

Or perhaps you consider these matters to be private: "Don't tell me how to run my relationship with God." No one has the right to question or intrude. Your personal standards are sacred. You know how much of the world you can tolerate without becoming intoxicated, and no one else can tell you when you've had too much.

Whatever the reason, this verse makes you uncomfortable. It invades your personal space. You're afraid if you get too close, these ten little words might come between you and the things in the world you enjoy. You're reluctant to discuss "worldliness" because then you might have to change.

Or perhaps you think 1 John 2:15 (and thus this book) doesn't apply to you. Maybe because of your age, or your position in the church, or your reputation for godliness, you think you're immune to worldliness. From all outward appearances you're anything but worldly—a solid member of your local church, an exemplary Christian who worships on Sunday and faithfully attends a small group. You've never committed a scandalous sin. In fact, you may be reading this book for someone else.

If we don't ignore 1 John 2:15 outright, we load it up with qualifications. We file down its edges with explanations. We dismiss it as applying only to those more "worldly" than us. We empty it of its authority, its meaning for our day-to-day lives.

"Do not love the world" is not, however, an outdated command or a remnant of an over-scrupulous tradition. It is *God's Word*. It comes straight from a loving heavenly Father to you and me. And it demands our urgent attention.

For if we ignore this verse, we are not merely guilty of presuming to manufacture our own Bible; we're in danger of being seduced by a fallen world.

And this threat is not confined to a specific group of people. We're all susceptible. There's no such thing as immunity based on age or position or ability to absorb the world without its affecting us. When it comes to worldliness, we're all at risk.

Don't believe me? Then let me introduce you to one of the most tragic characters in the Bible. Meet Demas.

Demas the Deserter

If ever there was a guy you'd have a hard time labeling "worldly," it would be Demas. Or so it seems.

As a close friend and traveling companion of the apostle Paul, Demas participated in spreading the gospel and strengthening the fledgling church throughout the Roman Empire. He left home and family to hit the long, dusty, and dangerous road with the itinerant apostle. He stood by Paul—likely at great personal risk—when the apostle landed in prison for the first time. We read of him sending greetings to the church in Colossae and to the Christian Philemon.

Here would appear to be a model Christian. A guy we would all admire, respect, and want to emulate.

Yet, a postscript in Paul's second letter to Timothy forms his epitaph: "Demas, in love with this present world, has deserted me" (2 Tim. 4:10).

Whoa. These words are like a kick to the gut. It's impossible to read them without feeling the sadness that was no doubt acutely felt by the apostle.

What a tragedy! A life wasted. A testimony ruined. The gospel maligned. For Demas, *in love with this present world*, not only deserted Paul and the saints—he deserted his Savior.

What happened? How did Demas go from passionate follower of Christ, close companion to the apostle, willing to risk all for the sake of the gospel, to *deserter*? Where did things go horribly wrong?

Before Demas deserted, he drifted.

It wasn't immediate. It wasn't obvious at first. He didn't go from disciple to deserter in a day. No, it was a gradual weakening, a subtle contaminating, and an eventual conforming to this world.

We all know a Demas—someone who, like a spiritual meteorite, burned bright with the love of Christ for a while, then suddenly (or so it seemed) faded from fellowship and turned his back on Christ, or fell into serious sin, leaving all to wonder what happened.

So often we're ignorant of the signs, the symptoms of worldliness. People can be attending church, singing the songs, apparently listening to the sermons—no different on the outside than they've always been.

But inside, that person is drifting. He sits in church but is not excited to be there. She sings songs without affection. He listens to preaching without conviction. She hears but does not apply.

A love for the world begins in the soul. It's subtle, not always immediately obvious to others, and often undetected by the people who are slowly succumbing to its lies.

It begins with a dull conscience and a listless soul. Sin does not grieve him like it once did. Passion for the Savior begins to cool. Affections grow dim. Excitement lessens for participating in the local church. Eagerness to evangelize starts to wane. Growth in godliness slows to a crawl.

In this way, the person who was once genuinely passionate for Christ—like Demas—is, over time, taken captive by sin.

It's simply one more step from apparent follower to deserter.

So, are you drifting?

"Oh, it's not serious," you say. "I've just been in a busy season. Yeah, I'm not as excited about the gospel or the Christian life as I used to be, but I'm fine. I'm still attending church. It's not like I've left God or anything. I've just been preoccupied lately. I'll get back on track soon."

Was there a time you were passionate for God, characterized by extravagant devotion and love for the Savior? Demas was like that once too.

What about now? Have you fallen in love with this present world?

Sadly, Christians are largely unaware of the peril. Because we've ignored verses such as 1 John 2:15, we've become completely desensitized to the clear and present danger of worldliness.

Distinctiveness Lost

Author James Hunter observes that we've "lost a measure of clarity" when it comes to how we relate to the world. He explains:

> Evangelicals still adhere to prohibitions against premarital, extramarital, and homosexual relations. But even here, the attitude toward those prohibitions has noticeably softened.

This softening, he points out, brings an inevitable result:

Worldliness

> Many of the distinctions separating Christian conduct
> from "worldly conduct" have been challenged if not alto-
> gether undermined. Even the words *worldly* and *worldliness*
> have, within a generation, lost most of their traditional
> meaning.[1]

We've softened. We've lost clarity. Within a generation, *worldly* and *worldliness* have lost most of their meaning, becoming mere clippings on the floor of our lives. The
distinctions between Christian and worldly conduct—once
so clear—have blurred beyond recognition. The slippery
slope from drifter to deserter has, in only a few years, grown
increasingly slick. This rapid loss of clarity has culminated
in crisis.

Today, the greatest challenge facing American evangeli-
cals is not persecution from the world, but seduction by the
world.

Unlike so many of our Christian brothers and sisters
who live in countries with oppressive regimes—where the
church is flourishing, by the way—we in America don't face
imminent threat to our families, livelihoods, and well-being
for professing faith in Christ. Our peril is far more obscure
and far more insidious. We aren't under attack from without;
we're decaying from within. Our success as ambassadors for
Christ, as witnesses of the life-changing power of the gospel,
hangs in the balance.

We've let down our guard against worldliness. And as a
love for the things of this world has infiltrated the church, it
has watered down and weakened our witness. It threatens to
silence our clarion call for repentance and faith in the Savior.

Charles Spurgeon, writing 150 years ago, nevertheless speaks poignantly to the problem in the church today: "I believe," he asserted, "that one reason why the church of God at this present moment has so little influence over the world is because the world has so much influence over the church."[2]

Further substantiating his claim, he calls history as a witness:

> Put your finger on any prosperous page in the Church's history, and I will find a little marginal note reading thus: "In this age men could readily see where the Church began and where the world ended." Never were there good times when the Church and the world were joined in marriage with one another. The more the Church is distinct from the world in her acts and in her maxims, the more true is her testimony for Christ, and the more potent is her witness against sin.[3]

The greater our difference from the world, the more true our testimony for Christ—and the more potent our witness against sin. But sadly, today, there's not much difference. The lines have blurred. The lack of clarity between the church and the world has undercut our testimony for Christ and undermined our witness against sin. In Spurgeon's words once again: "Worldliness is growing over the church; she is mossed with it."[4]

Is There a Difference?

Are the lines between Christian and worldly conduct blurry in your mind—and more importantly, in your life? To put it another way, is your lifestyle obviously different from that of the non-Christian?

Imagine I take a blind test in which my task is to identify the genuine follower of Jesus Christ. My choices are an unregenerate individual and you.

I'm given two reports detailing conversations, Internet activity, manner of dress, iPod playlists, television habits, hobbies, leisure time, financial transactions, thoughts, passions, and dreams.

The question is: Would I be able to tell you apart? Would I discern a difference between you and your unconverted neighbor, coworker, classmate, or friend?

Have the lines between Christian and worldly conduct in your life become so indistinguishable that there really is no difference at all?

If the difference is hard to detect, you may be in danger of drifting down the deserter's path with Demas.

In front of the deserter's path is a warning sign. It's 1 John 2:15: "Do not love the world or anything in the world."

This little book is a call to heed that warning. It's a passionate plea to a generation for whom the dangers of worldliness are perhaps more perilous than for any that has gone before.

But 1 John 2:15 isn't simply a "Do Not Enter" sign. These ten words (and the verses that follow) don't simply forbid worldliness, leaving us confused and unsure of where to go. They point the way to life in Christ. They help us see the pathway to what John Newton called "solid joys and lasting treasures."[5]

To understand this verse, you must first understand the

nature of warnings. They're not legalistic restrictions from an irritated God who doesn't want us to enjoy ourselves. And they aren't relics of a bygone era, irrelevant for us today. No, warnings are expressions of God's mercy and wisdom. They're given for our good, to protect us from sin and its consequences.

So let's ignore this warning no longer. Let's paste our Bibles back together and receive from God his wisdom and mercy found in 1 John 2:15.

Do Not Love the *What*?

First, let me be clear. The author of this book, John, is not calling for some kind of monastic separation from the world.

The "world" of 1 John 2:15 doesn't refer to the created order or to the blessings that come from living in a modern society, such as modern conveniences or medical and scientific advances. For God created the world and declared it "very good" (Gen. 1:31).

Nor does this verse refer to economic and social structures of society—our family, friends, vocation, field of study, government, or community. All of these are ordained by our heavenly Father. As David says, "The earth is the LORD's and the fullness thereof, the world and those who dwell therein" (Ps. 24:1).

And of course, we're supposed to love all men—not only our brothers and sisters in Christ but also those who are not Christians—because "God so loved the world" that he gave his Son (John 3:16). In fact, true love for God is demonstrated by a growing passion to tell others about his love. (That's why my good friend Jeff Purswell will conclude this book with a chapter on how to rightly love the world. Sound paradoxical? Keep reading to find out why it's anything but.)

So what is the "world" we are forbidden to love?

The world we're not to love is *the organized system of human civilization that is actively hostile to God and alienated from God.* The world God forbids us to love is the fallen world. Humanity at enmity with God. A world of arrogant, self-sufficient people seeking to exist apart from God and living in opposition to God. It's a world richly deserving of the righteous wrath of a holy God. Dead set against the gospel of Jesus Christ. This is the world we're forbidden to love.

While remaining *in* the world, we're not to become *like* the world. In the words of John Stott, we must be "neither conformed to [the world] nor contaminated by it."[6] But this sinful, fallen world is right in our face. Our affluent and technologically advanced society brings the world to our doorstep, into our homes, into our very presence. It baits our eyes and tickles our ears. We're saturated with media—bombarded by images on television and movie screens, and by music on our iPods. We have unlimited access—text messages on our cell phones, and Internet access on our laptops and hand-held devices. We enjoy countless options in clothes to wear, cars to buy, vacations to take, entertainment to view, music to listen to.

And obviously, while these things are not inherently evil, so often they're vehicles of a fallen world. They deliver endless opportunities to pursue pleasure without regard to God and his Word, endless opportunities to be seduced by this fallen world, to succumb to the sin of worldliness.

Every moment of every day we're making choices—

whether we realize it or not—between love for a world that opposes God and love for the risen Christ.

Defining Worldliness

Worldliness, then, is a love for this fallen world. It's loving the values and pursuits of the world that stand opposed to God. More specifically, it is *to gratify and exalt oneself to the exclusion of God*. It rejects God's rule and replaces it with our own (like creating our own Bibles). It exalts our opinions above God's truth. It elevates our sinful desires for the things of this fallen world above God's commands and promises.

"The goal of worldly people," observes Joel Beeke,

> is to move forward rather than upward, to live horizontally rather than vertically. They seek after outward prosperity rather than holiness. They burst with selfish desires rather than heartfelt supplications. If they do not deny God, they ignore and forget Him, or else they use Him only for their selfish ends. *Worldliness . . . is human nature without God.*[7]

Does that description sound familiar? Does it describe you?

What are your goals? Do they drive you *forward*—to financial security, more friends, successful kids, a certain position at work, learning a craft or trade? Or do they drive you *upward*—to obeying and glorifying God above all else? What gets you out of bed in the morning?

Try this: What dominates your mind and stirs your heart? Is it discontentment with your life? Longings for earthly pleasures? Does outward prosperity appeal to you more than growth in godliness? Or is your prayer life characterized by heartfelt supplications for God's will to be done and his kingdom to come?

Do you relate to God as if he exists to further your selfish ambitions or are you convinced that you exist to glorify him? Are you trying to live without God? Iain Murray describes this way of thinking:

> Worldliness is departing from God. It is a man-centred way of thinking; it proposes objectives which demand no radical breach with man's fallen nature; it judges the importance of things by the present and material results; it weighs success by numbers; it covets human esteem and wants no unpopularity; it knows no truth for which it is worth suffering; it declines to be "a fool for Christ's sake". Worldliness is the mind-set of the unregenerate. It adopts idols and is at war with God.[8]

Do you covet the esteem and crave the approval of those around you? Do you go to great lengths to avoid looking foolish or being rejected for your Christian faith? Do you consider present and material results more important than eternal reward? Have you departed from God and adopted idols instead? *Are you at war with God?*

These are tough questions, I know; but they are necessary if you're to discover whether you have been infected with the disease of worldliness.

The Root Issue

Mention worldliness, and you're sure to encounter opposing views among Christians. The conflict often reveals a wrong focus on externals.

Some people try to define worldliness as living *outside* a specific set of rules or conservative standards. If you listen to music with a certain beat, dress in fashionable clothes, watch movies with a certain rating, or indulge in certain luxuries of modern society, surely you must be worldly.

Others, irritated and repulsed by rules that seem arbitrary, react to definitions of worldliness, assuming it's impossible to define. Or they think legalism will inevitably be the result, so we shouldn't even try.

Ready for a surprise? Both views are wrong. For by focusing exclusively on externals or dismissing the importance of externals, we've missed the point. John—inspired by the Holy Spirit—takes the debate to a whole other level.

He takes it inside.

For that's where worldliness is. It exists in our hearts. Worldliness does not consist in outward behavior, though our actions can certainly be an *evidence* of worldliness within. But the real location of worldliness is internal. It resides in our hearts.

We see this by looking closely at the verse that follows: "For everything in the world—the cravings of sinful man, the lust of his eyes and the boasting of what he has and does—comes not from the Father but from the world" (1 John 2:16 NIV).

Notice that in enlarging upon what is "in the world," John doesn't say, "this particular mode of dress, this way of speaking, this music, these possessions." No, the essence of worldliness is in the *cravings* of sinful man, the *lust* of his eyes, and the *boasting* of what he has and does. "The 'worldly' characteristics of which this verse speaks," writes commentator David Jackman, "are in fact reactions going on inside us, as we contemplate the environment outside."[9]

Inspired by the Holy Spirit, John is wisely drawing our attention inside. The root issue is within. Before applying this discernment to the world around us, we must start with ourselves, for the root issue is internal, not environmental. We must learn to discern worldliness where it lurks—inside our hearts.

When Cravings Compete

With the phrase "cravings of sinful man," John is targeting our hearts. Although Christians have new hearts, remaining sin in our lives produces cravings that compete with God's supremacy in our hearts.

David Powlison, paraphrasing John Calvin, wrote, "The evil in our desires often lies not in what we want, but in the fact that we want it too much."[10] It's difficult to improve upon this insight. The "cravings of sinful man" are legitimate desires that have become false gods we worship. It's wanting too much the things of this fallen world.

A sinful craving is when a legitimate desire for financial success becomes a silent *demand* for financial success; an interest in clothes and fashion becomes a *preoccupation*; love of music morphs into an *obsession* with the hottest band; or the desire to enjoy a good movie becomes a *need* to see the latest blockbuster.

There may be nothing wrong with these desires in and of themselves; but when they dominate the landscape of our lives—when we *must* have them or else!—we've succumbed to idolatry and worldliness. And as Calvin says, our hearts are a perpetual factory of idols.[11] We're pumping out these things on a regular basis.

Or take John's next phrase, "the lust of his eyes." Our hearts may generate sinful cravings, but they can also be aroused by what we see. The eyes themselves are a precious gift from God. But they're also windows into our soul, providing opportunities for us not simply to observe but to covet. Please don't limit this to sexual sin; practically anything we see can stimulate greed in our souls.

So what are you captivated by? Really, what do you think about most often, what images have the power to arouse your interest? It's probably whatever is coming to mind right now. And we must ask ourselves, what value does it have?

If you're more excited about the release of a new movie or video game than about serving in the local church, if you're drawn to people more because of their physical attractiveness or personality than their character, if you're impressed by Hollywood stars or professional athletes regardless of their lack of integrity or morality, then you've been seduced by this fallen world.

And finally, "the boasting of what he has and does." We're all so familiar with this temptation, are we not? We find ourselves so easily tempted to take pride in our work, our talents or abilities, our physical appearance, possessions, or accomplishments.

We might be too polite to boast aloud, but secretly we revel in what we have and what we've done. We think we're significant because of our assets and achievements, and we want others to notice. How do you define yourself? How does your profile read? How do you want to be known?

Do you think of yourself as "the guy with the impressive title" or "the most attractive girl in the room"? Are you the person with the Ivy-League education or the fancy car or the beautifully decorated home? Is your hobby or talent or career the most important thing about you? Or is it even your spouse or your kids—their successes and accomplishments?

We must not define ourselves by, or boast in, anything we possess or accomplish in this world. Instead we should identify with Christ and his definition of greatness: the humble, the servant.

The cravings of sinful man . . . the lust of his eyes . . . the boasting of what he has and does. We don't often identify these root issues of the sin of worldliness. And once again, *clip, clip, clip*—1 John 2:15 is left out of "our" version of the Bible.

Where There Is No Future

After highlighting the godlessness of the things of the world, John then exposes their futility: "The world and its desires pass away, but the man who does the will of God lives forever" (1 John 2:17 NIV). The verse is clear: these things don't last. They pass away.

My friend, I don't want you to waste your life pursuing things that won't last. I don't want you to have what John Owen describes as "living affections to dying things."[12]

There's no future in worldliness. None. This world is temporary and superficial, and it doesn't satisfy. Oh, I know, the world sparkles, the world dazzles. I know because I've been there. I immersed myself in the world. I passionately pursued everything it had to offer. And what did I discover? It didn't deliver as advertised. It deceived me. What it did deliver were unadvertised consequences I wasn't informed of and didn't anticipate. For sin carries with it the seeds of dissatisfaction and destruction.

The things of this world—when compared to pleasing God and eternal life, when informed by an eternal perspective—will be exposed as being worthless. But there is a future in godliness, and for all who do the will of God. They, by contrast, will live forever.

What Matters Most

How about you? Which will you choose? Will you pursue the deceptive, temporary pleasures of worldliness? Or do the will of God, which contains the promise of eternal life?

Maybe, as you read this chapter, you realize you're drifting. Or maybe you're in headlong pursuit of worldliness. You may realize your affection for the things of this world is strong, your love for Christ weak.

And you feel trapped, entangled in the net of worldliness. Despair sets in. Condemnation comes to call. *You'll never change. You'll never be able to give up the things of the world you love so much. You might as well not even try. You're beyond hope.*

Yes, resisting worldliness requires strenuous effort. It's an inside problem and hard heart-work will be needed to effectively cut it out. And it's a lifelong battle. We must resist its influence until our dying breath.

However, this isn't a battle fought by sheer willpower or teeth-gritting self-denial. We can't overcome worldliness on our own. We are not sufficient. A much greater strength is required.

But take heart! All that we need to overcome worldliness has been provided for us.

The antidote to worldliness is the cross of Jesus Christ.

Only through the power of the cross of Christ can we successfully resist the seduction of the fallen world. The Savior's death on the cross is what makes possible forgiveness of sin and provides power to overcome sin. And the cross is the attraction that draws our hearts away from the empty and deadly pleasures of worldliness.

If you want to begin immediately to weaken the influence of worldliness in your life, take the sound advice from that great physician of the soul, John Owen:

> When someone sets his affections upon the cross and the love of Christ, he crucifies the world as a dead and undesirable thing. The baits of sin lose their attraction and disappear. Fill your affections with the cross of Christ and you will find no room for sin.[13]

Do you want the world to lose its appeal? Then crowd out worldliness by filling your affections with the cross of Christ. Crucify the world as a dead and undesirable thing by meditating on the love of the Savior. Resist the bait of the world by gazing at the wondrous cross. For it is "the cross of our Lord Jesus Christ," wrote Paul, "by which the world has been crucified to me, and I to the world" (Gal. 6:14).

Charles Spurgeon urged us to "dwell where the cries of Calvary can be heard."[14] If we will do this, then the things of this world will indeed "grow strangely dim in the light of His glory and grace."[15]

What should consume our thoughts and affections is not resisting worldliness but the glory and grace of God revealed at the cross. We must take the sin of worldliness seriously, to be sure; that's why we wrote this book. But its eradication is not an end in itself. Resisting worldliness is absolutely vital but not ultimately most significant.

Jesus Christ is most important. We must fight worldliness because it dulls our affections for Christ and distracts our attention from Christ. Worldliness is so serious because Christ is so glorious.

While resisting worldliness is this book's theme, exalting Christ is its aim. That's why I've closed this chapter, and why we'll eventually close this book, surveying the wondrous cross on which the Prince of Glory died.

Meditate on the cross. Consider the wonders of the Savior who died for sinners and rose victorious over sin and death. Dwell where the cries of Calvary are louder than the clamor of the world.

Chapter Two

God, My Heart, and Media

Craig Cabaniss

CONSIDER A DAY IN THE LIFE of a typical American adult. The waking moments begin with the radio alarm reporting weather, traffic, and headlines. Breakfast is gulped down with a side of business news and features from the morning newspaper.

Then the commute to work, where the companion for the drive is a radio talk show host lathered into a political frenzy or a shock jock whose tongue releases a barrage of crude humor.

At the office, checking e-mail presents opportunities throughout the morning for a bit of extracurricular web-surfing to shop for a birthday gift, check out a favorite blog, and catch up on the latest celebrity news. Lunch in the break-room is spent connecting with a favorite sports magazine while a TV talk show blares overhead, showcasing the latest claimants to fleeting fame. Back in the cubicle's afternoon boredom, virtual adventure can be found on an Internet video game offering a quest for world domination.

When the work grind ceases, the drive home provides a reprieve from thinking and a nostalgic unwinding as the oldies stream in on satellite radio. The trip down memory lane is interrupted by a stop at soccer practice to pick up a young daughter who eagerly buckles up and warmly greets the Disney character coming to life on the DVD screen that descends in the backseat.

After a welcome-home kiss from the wife—and a friendlier kiss from the dog—comes the irresistible beckoning to collapse into the La-Z-Boy, grab the remote, and scan all three hundred digital cable channels to take the edge off the workday weariness. Following dinner, the TV illuminates the family room as all gather to enjoy the hottest sitcoms, reality shows, and crime dramas.

The day concludes with a drift into slumber to the soothing voice of a newscaster recapping headlines on the bedroom TV.

For most Americans, media is the omnipresent backdrop of life. Even if you don't find yourself in every scene of the previous day-in-the-life scenario, you're nevertheless surrounded. Whether at home, in the car, at the store, in a restaurant, or even at the gas station (I've seen CNN piped in via a small screen built into the pump), the perpetual media lifeline continues. We're never beyond its ubiquitous reach. We're so engulfed that media seems like a second atmosphere; in fact one author terms our cultural surroundings the "mediasphere."[1] We give no more thought to it than we do to the air we breathe.

But give thought to it we must. As followers of Christ, we cannot afford to take lightly the media's pervasive presence in our lives.

Think about the power of video entertainment, for

instance. Whether viewed on computer, a portable player, or a traditional TV set, television and film are without peer in their cultural influence. Ken Myers, an astute Christian observer of popular culture, notes that television is not only "the dominant medium of popular culture" but also "the single most significant shared reality in our entire society." He compares television's impact to that of Christianity centuries ago, when "Christendom" defined the Western world:

> Not all citizens of Christendom were Christians, but all understood it, all were influenced by its teaching. . . . I can think of no entity today capable of such a culturally unifying role except television. In television, we live and move and have our being.[2]

Similarly, pastor Kent Hughes offers this alarming appraisal:

> Today the all-pervasive glow of the television set is the single most potent influence and control in Western culture. Television has greater power over the lives of most Americans than any educational system, government, or church.[3]

But it's not enough to acknowledge the dominant, nearly godlike authority exercised over our culture by TV, the Internet, and the rest of the media. We must evaluate the content of media messages and the consequences of their influence.

We begin by recognizing that the media's messages are nothing new. Essentially, our world puts forward the same allurements that the apostle John's world did some two thousand years ago: "the desires of the flesh and the desires of the eyes and pride in possessions" (1 John 2:16). Christians in John's day didn't have the Internet, cable television, or iPods, but the desires of the flesh have been around since the fall. To be sure, the packaging and delivery of the world's offerings have advanced technologically, but their substance has remained as primitive as a talking serpent. Christians of all ages have been required to soberly assess the temptations found in the surrounding culture and to respond in a God-glorifying way. We are no different. As this book's subtitle points out, our calling as Christians involves resisting the seduction of a fallen world.

This chapter will focus on television and film media, though the principles are relevant for evaluating all forms of media, all of which to some degree embody values of our fallen world. If we're faithfully to resist the ever-present "desires of the flesh and the desires of the eyes and pride in possessions," we'll need to sharpen our biblical discernment and wisely evaluate our media intake, for the glory of God.

Watching Unwatchingly

Many of us don't think about actively filtering our viewing. As long as we avoid the obvious traps such as pornography, we don't consider deliberate evaluation necessary. Though we may faithfully apply the Scriptures in other areas of life, we may not consciously think about how God's Word applies to our entertainment choices.

All too often, we think about neither what we watch nor how much. Our watching is just inevitable. We watch by habit. We watch because we're bored. We unwatchingly watch as the TV stays on for background noise.

We watch alone or with others. We gather with friends on Friday night and rent a DVD because there's nothing else to do.

We watch because others watch. Everyone at school or at work is talking about a popular movie. It's a must see—so we must see it. Without researching its content, without thinking about its effect on our hearts, without comparing an evening at the movies with other options, we go, and we watch.

Please don't misunderstand. I'm not saying it's wrong to watch television, rent a DVD, surf the Internet, or spend an evening at the cinema. The hazard is *thoughtless* watching. Glorifying God is an intentional pursuit. We don't accidentally drift into holiness; rather, we mature gradually and purposefully, one choice at a time. In the Christian walk, we can't just step onto the right path and figure all is well. Christian discipleship is a lifelong journey consisting of a series of countless steps. Each step matters, and thus our viewing habits matter.

A lifestyle of careless viewing should concern us. At best, careless viewing reveals an ignorance of the media's power of temptation. It probably indicates a degree of laziness as well—and we can't afford to be lazy in what our minds absorb. Biblical discernment involves critical thinking, which often leads to costly action. It's true that we grow in sanctification by God's grace, but this doesn't deny that our growth involves work. To mature, we need engaged minds asking biblically informed questions about the media's messages and methods. What's more, we need perseverance to travel against the cultural current.

To change the metaphor, detecting and avoiding temptation is a battle; every time we pick up the remote or glance at the movie listings or go online, we take up arms. Ken Myers describes this battle in strong terms:

> I believe that the challenge of living with popular culture may well be as serious for modern Christians as persecution and plagues were for the saints of earlier centuries. . . . Enemies that come loudly and visibly are usually much easier to fight than those that are undetectable.[4]

It may seem that Myers exaggerates the danger. Pop culture as deadly as persecution and plagues?

But I think he's right. When it comes to waging the war of sanctification, severe trial usually alerts us to battle, rousing us to our need for God. Popular culture, especially entertainment media, often lulls us to ignore our battle with the flesh.

In this conflict, how many Christians are waving the white flag of surrender by disengaging their discernment when it comes to media? But passivity is no option. We're called to live purposefully. That means we must watch on purpose and resist the lifestyle of passive viewing.

Watching with Immunity?

Unlike those who watch thoughtlessly, many Christians recognize the tempting influence of media yet assume they're immune from danger. They end up watching just like everyone else.

"After all," they'll argue, "I'm not going to watch a murder on TV and then go out and murder someone." This misses the point. Our sanctification aspirations should be loftier than avoiding murder. Just because we don't instantly mimic all we see doesn't mean our hearts aren't negatively affected by the programs or films we watch. Tugging like a subtle undertow below the surface, the media can tempt us to drift toward love of the world.

Drift toward worldliness may be slow, its symptoms not immediately apparent. This drift is usually a sign of a dulling conscience. The conscience doesn't function like a light switch—one moment the lights are on, then everything is dark with a flip of the switch. Instead, the sensitivity of our conscience dulls over time as it is resisted or ignored. Paul charges young Timothy to "wage the good warfare" by holding on to a good conscience, and warns him that rejecting a good conscience can lead to shipwrecking one's faith (1 Tim. 1:18–20). Over time a good conscience that once was sensitive to the holiness of God and the conviction of the Spirit can become seared (1 Tim. 4:2), losing all feeling.

The drift toward worldliness is subtle, gradual, and internal. And if we assume we're immune to it, that's a sure sign the drift has begun.

The media has great power to influence, but most people—both Christians and unbelievers—presuppose that their worldview, desires, and opinions are safe from media sway. We're convinced we're beyond reach. How revealing, then, that advertisers spend $215 billion annually just on television commercials. These marketing dollars are not charity gifts; our thinking is influenced by what we watch, and advertisers know it.

We also tend to think of ourselves as minimally exposed to media, especially compared to everyone else. In a Roper survey that reveals as much about human nature as it does about media consumption, 96 percent of people polled claimed they watched less television than the average person. You don't need a sophisticated statistical analysis of that survey to realize a lot of us don't have a clue about our viewing habits.

These examples illustrate what the Scripture teaches about our hearts. They're sinful, and as a result, we're prone to self-deception. "The heart is deceitful above all things, and desperately sick; who can understand it?" (Jer. 17:9). We're more easily tempted than we know or are willing to admit.

The Bible teaches that the battle is not "out there." The real monster isn't Hollywood or a beast residing in a plasma screen. He's not lurking behind the curtain in the movie theater. He's much closer. He's *us*. Our battle is with the flesh. "For the desires of the flesh are against the Spirit, and the desires of the Spirit are against the flesh, for these are opposed to each other, to keep you from doing the things you want to do" (Gal. 5:17).

If we watch, we must watch with this in mind: our hearts are deceitful, and our flesh will be tempted. Paul's warning to the Corinthians is fitting: "Therefore let anyone who thinks that he stands take heed lest he fall" (1 Cor. 10:12).

We're commanded to "not be conformed to this world"

(Rom. 12:2), but such conformity is the inevitable pathway for those who watch freely with the delusion of immunity.

The *L* Word

No discussion of media standards gets far before someone cries, "Legalism!" Any teaching that advocates some level of viewing standards will be stereotyped in some quarters as a compromising of Christian liberty.

Such stereotyping works both ways, of course. The one advocating higher standards can just as easily broad-brush all detractors as "worldly" or "licentious." Meanwhile we conveniently place ourselves in the center: all those with stricter entertainment standards than ours are legalistic, while anyone who's more lenient is worldly.

Legalism, however, is not a matter of having more rigorous rules. It's far more lethal than that. It strikes at the very core of our relationship with God. As C. J. Mahaney explains:

> Legalism is seeking to achieve forgiveness from God and acceptance by God through obedience to God. In other words, a legalist is anyone who behaves as if they can earn God's approval and forgiveness through personal performance.[5]

Do we risk legalism by establishing personal viewing standards? Absolutely! But the risk doesn't lie in having standards; it lies in our motivation. The question is not, "Should we view selectively?" but "*Why* do we view selectively?" We must not seek to earn God's favor by watching or not watching certain programs. Our forgiveness from God and acceptance by God are based upon the gospel—we're already approved because of the death, burial, and resurrection of Christ. Therefore, our obedience springs from gratitude for the gospel.

Legalism is a heart condition that can easily affect our media viewing (or lack of viewing) just as it can color any other activity. Legalism can taint our Bible reading, praying, witnessing, eating, sleeping, lovemaking, working, recreating, joking, shopping—we can be legalistic about anything! The solution is not necessarily lowering our standards. It *is* necessarily raising our understanding of and response to the glorious grace of God.

Another objection to setting viewing standards is a fear of isolationism. Some will argue that our evangelism is compromised when we detach ourselves from our culture, and that we're called instead to engage it. There's truth to this claim; but when "engage the culture" is a euphemism for "watch whatever everyone else is watching," our witness is weakened, not strengthened. It's foolish to think the gospel will spread more powerfully if we hide its transforming effect in our lives. While we should celebrate any genuine concern for reaching out to the lost, we should be suspect of any approach advocating broad cultural accommodation when it comes to entertainment.

Recently, a lady in our church communicated to me her resistance to the idea of curbing media consumption; she believed that viewing current TV programs and movies enabled her to better relate to the lost. But she came to question her own reasoning: "Am I lowering my standards to stay up with our culture while not really reaching anyone by doing so?" I respect her for her humility and honesty. She asks a discerning question.

In reality, it isn't necessary to be a media glutton to share the gospel effectively. We can meaningfully relate with people in our culture without immersing ourselves in the latest entertainments. We can be aware of popular culture without being captive to it. Our personal and corporate relevance and witness won't be hindered at all by applying biblical standards to our media intake.

This leads us to explore a grace-motivated approach to media consumption. We begin, most appropriately, with God.

Living *Coram Deo*

Coram Deo is a short Latin phrase packing a potent punch: "before the face of God." All aspects of our existence—from private thoughts to public words and actions—are lived out before his face. Properly regarded, living *coram Deo* arouses our fear of God. The person who's aware that God is seated front-and-center and watching everything will fear the Lord. And that's good, for "the fear of the LORD is the beginning of knowledge" (Prov. 1:7).

The fear of God is our starting place; it's not the graduate school of Christian discipleship. Fearing God is where we begin in our search for knowledge and wisdom. The fool, by contrast, is one whose governing mindset excludes the reality of God (Ps. 14:1).

What does all this have to do with our media use? Put bluntly, it means we surf the Internet, listen to the radio, watch television, or rent a DVD *in God's presence*. We make our choices—all our choices—with God's holy face in view. It's not the gaze of our pastor, parent, fellow small group member, or unbelieving neighbor that matters most. We're accountable to God in all things, including our entertainment.

Wayne Wilson brings home this sobering truth: "We are accountable to God, and the label of 'art' on human expression does not remove this accountability in the slightest way."[6]

God is holy, and we are not. *Coram Deo*, we realize we're in trouble—our eyes have lusted, our imaginations have trespassed, our time has been squandered. We must run to the cross where God's holiness and mercy intersect decisively. *Coram Deo*, we find grace. Grace that forgives. Grace that empowers us to change. Grace that leads us to desire and pursue obedience. Any discussion of biblical obedience, including entertainment guidelines, must spring from a robust understanding of grace.

Grace-motivated Obedience

No book in Scripture provides any clearer model for grace-motivated obedience than Ephesians. We'll consider a number of verses found in Ephesians 5:1–14, but in order to understand that passage better, we must first take into account the overall outline of the book.

In the first three chapters of Ephesians, Paul passionately portrays God's grace. At points he's led to uncontained, blissful worship as he describes the gospel: we were chosen before the foundation of the world; we were graciously redeemed through Christ's blood; we were saved as a gift of God and not of works; we who were once far off are now joined with God's people. On and on, Paul recounts what God has done. Consumed with God's accomplishment for his people in Christ, these three chapters are a masterpiece of grace.

It's telling that Paul doesn't begin giving commands until chapter 4. He first wants to make sure we "get it": what *God* has done *for us* must be clear before discussing what we're to do for him. Then in 4:1 he urges the Ephesians "to walk in a manner worthy of the calling to which you have been called." Throughout chapter 4 he describes how that looks within the church, while in chapter 5 he describes how it looks in relation to the world. Without question, God calls us to a high standard of purity in these verses, a standard permanently tethered to the work of Christ.

Take a moment and read Ephesians 5:1–14. Seriously. Are you reading Ephesians 5:1–14? (I've been told most readers will never stop at this point and read Ephesians 5:1–14, but I don't think you're like most readers. So I'll just wait while you read it . . .)

In these verses Paul demonstrates what it means to live life resisting the seduction of a fallen world. These verses may not speak directly of sitcoms, romantic movies, or music videos, but they do speak to the themes of much of our modern entertainment. At the heart of this passage is this summons: "Walk as children of light (for the fruit of light is found in all that is good and right and true), and try to discern what is pleasing to the Lord" (5:8–10). Here is a call to God-pleasing discernment. God makes clear that all that is "good and right and true" pleases him.

Applied to our entertainment, God-pleasing discernment involves remembering his grace to us in the death and resurrection of our Savior, then responding to his grace with a heart eager to please him by taking pleasure in what is good and right and true. Discerning what pleases the Lord requires critically evaluating media content at all times.

Sometimes it's easy for me to sit back and watch without cautious evaluation. At other times, I watch on high alert. Interestingly, I've found that I reserve my highest scrutiny for infomercials. My discernment spikes off the charts when these modern snake oil sellers start talking. Though I'm not a fan of this programming and certainly wouldn't gather my wife and kids around the tube for a family night of popcorn and infomercials, I must admit that while channel surfing I've landed on them from time to time, and I've watched. Like a rubbernecker inching past a wreck on the freeway, I guess I'm guilty of a morbid curiosity.

When I watch an infomercial, I'm anything but a passive viewer. I aggressively evaluate all claims. In fact, I'm compelled to carry on a loud conversation with the spokesperson. "No way!" I laugh. "Get out of here!" When some Ken doll tells me that only 30 seconds a day with the "Gut Buster 3000" gave him perfectly sculpted abs, and that this new washboard of a belly has changed his life in every way, I don't buy it for a second! I tell him, "What about the fact that as a fitness guru you exercise all day for a living? What about the fact that you eat nothing but vitamin supplements and lawn clippings? What about the fact that your genes and my genes are about as similar as Gene Simmons and Gene Kelly?"

Because the infomercial claims are exaggerated, the bait

isn't so enticing. I know the worm's a fake. I know chiseled abs won't change my life. No one would even see them except my wife, who doesn't seem too troubled over this issue. Thankfully our marriage covenant is tighter than my abs.

We should apply this same level of discernment whenever we're exposed to entertainment media. If we don't realize that their claims are false, the bait will indeed appear enticing. Obviously, infomercials are a different genre than primetime TV or film, but they each communicate a worldview, a philosophy of what is good, right, and true.

Usually, the message of a TV show or film is far more subtle than an advertising spokesmodel sporting a cheesy grin and proclaiming, "With these new abs, life's great!" The more subtle the message, however, the more crucial the need for perceptive viewing. And if we fail to be discerning or neglect to watch wisely, we end up with something much worse than cheap exercise gear collecting dust in the garage. We end up hooked by the bait of "the desires of the flesh and the desires of the eyes and pride in possessions."

In Ephesians 5, God not only calls us to discern what is pleasing to him, but he also plainly identifies what is displeasing. As we move through these verses, we find that Paul's world and ours share much in common. The Ephesians, like us, live in a dark world where sexual immorality, greed, idolatry, and impurity are "normal." But for those transformed by the gospel, who were once darkness but are now light (5:8), life is not culturally "normal." We're no longer to take part in "the unfruitful works of darkness" (5:11); rather, we're to live in the light as those who have experienced new life in

Jesus Christ. Now that we're different people, we're to live different lives.

Though not exhaustive, this passage does provide guidance for honoring God with our media intake. We start with the mandate to avoid impurity in light of Christ's love and sacrifice (5:1–2).

Watch What They Do

"But among you there must not be even a hint of sexual immorality, or of any kind of impurity, or of greed, because these are improper for God's holy people" (Eph. 5:3 NIV).

It's hard to imagine a stronger statement than "not even a hint." Not even a hint of immorality. Not even a hint of impurity. Not even a hint of greed. I wonder how our viewing habits would be adjusted if this verse was constantly scrolled across the bottom of our television screens like the CNN news headlines.

We don't have to look far to find television programs or films that feature more than a hint of sexual impurity. "But watching isn't doing," someone may argue. "Isn't the sin in the act?" Yet these verses condemn sinful desires as well. The term "greed" (v. 3) is also translated "covetousness" (ESV). In his commentary on Ephesians, Peter T. O'Brien offers the translation "sexually covetous" because covetousness is a desire for some*thing* or some*one* that God has not provided. Even a hint of sexual longing for someone other than a spouse is covetousness. We must ask, "Does this program or film tempt me with sexually impure thoughts or actions?" If so, there must not be "even a hint" of this on our screen.

The passage doesn't soften as it progresses: "Take no part

in the unfruitful works of darkness, but instead expose them. For it is shameful even to speak of the things that they do in secret" (5:11–12). If sexual sin is shameful and shouldn't even be spoken with specifics, then obviously it shouldn't be broadcast—high-definition and surround-sound—into our living rooms. We take part in "the unfruitful works of darkness" when entertaining ourselves with things our holy God despises.

How far do we take this? Doesn't the Bible itself record sexual sin that would be forbidden reading under these guidelines? If a film's plotline contains an adulterous affair, should we avoid the movie? What if the adultery takes place off camera?

These are good questions. The reference in verse 12 to things done "in secret" is clarifying as we apply this passage. It's one thing for a film to include sexual sin as part of the story but quite another to dramatize the act for the camera. Sexuality shouldn't be used gratuitously to titillate the audience. We live in a fallen world where fallen people sin sexually, and as an accurate reflection of our world, we'd expect some art to include themes like immorality or infidelity. However, the visual and verbal details of immorality should remain "in secret."

Along these lines, author Wayne Wilson makes these beneficial comments:

> Rather than giving us the details of depraved acts, good art can reveal the depraved heart through well written stories, enlightening us to the evil we may find within ourselves. We learn nothing by being made aware of the details of

sexual acts or rape. We do learn by seeing the ruinous effects of pride, bitterness, anger, and yes, even lusts, which can be shown without the lurid details.[7]

If a film or program does include off-screen impurity as a legitimate part of the story line, we still must ask, "How is the impurity represented?" In our passage Paul warns, "Let no one deceive you with empty words, for because of these things [sexual immorality, impurity, covetousness] the wrath of God comes upon the sons of disobedience" (5:6). Whenever we watch sin portrayed without consequences, we're subject to deception. Sin—sexual sin in particular— is often glamorized and sensationalized in media. But like the infomercial, the claims are deceptive. They're "empty words." Pleasure without guilt. Ecstasy without relational destruction. And worst of all, sin without judgment. Filling our minds with these media deceptions dulls our sensitivity to God's holy hatred of sin.

Under the old covenant, God prescribed stoning for adultery: "If a man commits adultery with the wife of his neighbor, both the adulterer and the adulteress shall surely be put to death" (Lev. 20:10). If we're honest, we have to admit this seems extreme. Why does it? Probably because we don't have a healthy view of the blazing holiness of God, who is "of purer eyes than to see evil and cannot look at wrong" (Hab. 1:13). It may also be because we've seen adulterers go on to live happily ever after. We've watched innumerable romantic comedies where two beautiful individuals fall for each other in the most unlikely way. They enjoy beautiful, illicit sex and then stroll off hand in hand to a beautiful life together as the credits roll. In reality, sexual immorality is anything but beautiful—no matter how attractive the actors, how sentimental the plot, how touching the dialogue, or how romantic the soundtrack.

God commands us not to be deceived and reminds us that his dreadful wrath awaits the sexually immoral (5:6). Immorality must never be portrayed as appealing, alluring, or safe. When it is, we're to avoid such depictions.

Watch What They Say

In today's American church culture, especially among young adults, it's unpopular to advocate restraint on speech. In fact, many of today's younger leaders take pride in their liberty to use terms and expressions (even in the pulpit) from popular culture that would have been assigned to the "bad word" list in previous generations. I understand their quarrel with a moralistic approach to holiness that seems to ignore the heart and that equates maturity with steering clear of certain so-called bad words. I'm not advocating that type of skin-deep piety. However, Scripture is clear. Our words matter.

Grace-motivated obedience extends beyond our thoughts and deeds: "Let there be no filthiness nor foolish talk nor crude joking, which are out of place, but instead let there be thanksgiving" (Eph. 5:4). Paul's reference to "filthiness" has to do with obscenity. Vulgar, lewd, perverted, or off-color speech is out of place. "Foolish talk" describes the speech of fools. Biblically, a fool is someone who's lacking not in intelligence but in the fear of God. Foolish talk mocks or ignores the moral law of God. In this context, "crude joking" describes humor with sexual overtones. Double entendre relating to immorality, perverse humor, and just plain dirty jokes has no place for one who has been made new in Christ.

If we're forbidden to speak with filthiness and crude sexual humor, we're equally prohibited from listening to it when we have a choice. Just because we don't personally tell obscene jokes, we're not off the hook when we plop down our cash at the box office and hire someone to entertain us on the big screen with gratuitous immoral humor. Sometimes people will evaluate a film, saying, "There's no sex. Just some crude jokes, and that's no big deal." On the contrary, this passage says crude joking is "out of place" (5:4).

Such filthy talk or crude humor isn't limited to the programs and films we watch. It can also surface as an Internet temptation. The same biblical guidelines are to govern our speech when we participate in online "conversations" through e-mail, blogs, or social networking web sites like MySpace or Facebook.

Filthiness, foolish talk, and crude joking are "out of place"—they're forbidden not because they're on some arbitrary "banned words" list, but because they reflect the heart and attitude of those who disregard God and his Word. Living in a way that's distinct from the world means speaking in a way that's distinct from the world. Grace changes us from the inside out, and a changed heart will lead to a changed vocabulary.

Therefore, "instead" of perverse language, "let there be thanksgiving" (5:4). Thanksgiving characterizes the believer's new vocabulary. Here's the point: we shouldn't crudely joke about sex. We should thank God for it. As John Stott explains,

> Christians should dislike and avoid vulgarity . . . not because we have a warped view of sex, and are either ashamed or afraid of it, but because we have a high and holy view of it as being in its right place God's good gift, which we do not want to see cheapened. All God's gifts, including sex, are subjects for thanksgiving, rather than for joking. To joke about them is bound to degrade them; to thank God for them is the way to preserve their worth as the blessings of a loving creator.[8]

Our culture degrades God's gift of sex in countless ways. This is nowhere more obvious than in sitcoms, stand-up routines, late-night talk shows, and comedy movies. In light of God's holiness, immorality should lead to weeping, not laughing. God is not by any means a prude; he created sex to be enjoyed to the fullest in marriage. We cultivate a high view of both God and sex when we thank him for it; we demean both God and sex when we obscenely joke about it.

Any sexual impurity fails the standard of what is "proper among saints" (5:3). A "saint" is someone set apart through the gospel. Walking in a manner worthy of the gospel means we're to watch what we watch. We're not only to avoid impurity in thought, speech, and action but also to steer clear of impure entertainment as well. Christ died for the impure sins of impure people so that we may live as new people testifying to the transforming power of the gospel.

Viewer Discretion Advised

Having unpacked some of Paul's instruction for discerning "what is pleasing to the Lord" in Ephesians 5:1–14, we now broaden our discussion and consider how to further apply biblical discernment to our media consumption.

When deciding on the appropriateness of a particular program or film, we often make a judgment based on its rating. However, simply knowing what it's rated does not mean we've applied thorough biblical discernment. While offering some help, the ratings system doesn't use biblical criteria to evaluate the content of films. And no ratings system can answer questions regarding the stewardship of our time or the motive of our heart in viewing. We need more than a rating if we're to honor God through our viewing. We need an evaluation process that takes into account our time and our motive, as well as offering a biblical benchmark for measuring content.

The following application questions can help in discerning the benefit of watching a particular movie or program. I've also included some related questions regarding Internet usage.

Time Questions

• Am I skipping or delaying something important in order to watch this now?

• What are my other social/entertainment options besides watching television or going out to see a movie?

• How much time have I already spent on media today?

• How much time have I spent surfing the Internet? How much time have I spent blogging or maintaining an online presence through social network sites?

• In the last week, how much time have I spent on the spiritual disciplines, building relationships, or serving in my local church compared to time spent consuming media?

• After investing the time to view this, will I look back on it as time well spent?

Heart Questions

• Why do I want to watch this program or film? What do I find entertaining about it?

• Am I seeking to escape from something I should be facing by watching this? Am I seeking comfort or relief that can be found only in God?

• What sinful temptations will this program or film present?

• Do I secretly want to view something in it that's sinful? Am I deceiving myself by saying, "I'll fast-forward through the bad parts"?

• Similarly, am I telling myself, "I'll just visit this web site once, and I won't click on any other links I find there"?

• Am I watching because I'm bored or lazy? If so, what does that reveal about my heart?

• Am I watching simply because others are? Am I trying to be relevant or to fit in?

• How have my online relationships impacted my face-to-face relationships? How has my online activity impacted my soul? For better or worse?

• What motivates me to create and maintain a blog, MySpace, or Facebook presence? Am I attempting to impress others? Am I being prideful, slanderous, deceitful, or self-righteous?

Content Questions

• What worldview or philosophy of life does this program or film present? What's the view of man's nature? What's the view of sin? Is sin identified as such? What's the view of God-ordained authority figures? And how do these views relate to God's view?

• What does this program or film glamorize? What is valued or considered important?

• Who are the heroes of the story? Why are they heroic?

• Is sin shown as having negative consequences? Or is sin glorified or rewarded? Is sin presented in an appealing or seductive way?

• What is humorous in this work? How are people made fun of? What is mocked?

• Does violence appear as a natural part of the story, or is it used gratuitously to entertain?

• What's the sexual content? Is there nudity? Sensual or seductive dress? Are there images, language, or humor that are sexually impure?

• Is sinful self-sufficiency honored? Are the heroic characters concerned for others or merely for themselves?

• Does the program or film portray materialism as "the good life"?

• Would seeing this help me better understand God's world? Would it help me understand my surrounding culture better without tempting me to sinful compromise?

• Will I benefit in any way from viewing this program or visiting this web site?

• Does its content or artistry reflect truth, beauty, or goodness?

• Online, do I communicate graciously, patiently, and humbly? Do I use crude or arrogant speech? Is my speech consistent with the gospel, or does it reflect worldliness?

After reading these questions, you may get the feeling that practicing discernment is a lot of work. It can be, but it's worth the careful deliberation because the goal is lofty: discerning what pleases the Lord.

By asking these sorts of questions, we may find that although a certain program is acceptable, spending the time to watch it may not be beneficial. Think about Paul's counsel to the Corinthians: "'All things are lawful,' but not all things are helpful. 'All things are lawful,' but not all things build up" (1 Cor. 10:23). One author offers the following application of this verse:

> What if we began to test all our media consumption from the nightly news to our entertainment programs to our video rentals? And furthermore, what if the standard was looking for what might be beneficial instead of what might simply be permissible?[9]

On the other hand, we may have the discretionary time to view something, but the content may be questionable. Whenever possible, we should research the content of a program or film before watching. (For example, www.pluggedinonline.com is a helpful resource to preview film content from a Christian worldview.) To be forewarned is to be forearmed: when we're informed, we can make selective choices to avoid temptation and sin.

Once we walk through a process deciding "if" we should view and "what" we should view, we also want to think about "how" we should view. How can we view entertainment media for the glory of God?

View Proactively

Viewing for God's glory requires responding to temptations as they arise. This means we press the remote, click the mouse, or walk out of the theater when we discern that our entertainment displeases the Lord. We must resist the temptation to think, "There's nothing else to watch," or "I'm only looking for a moment," or "It would be stupid to waste the money I spent to see this." Watching *coram Deo* leads to acting *coram Deo*.

When writing to the Thessalonians, Paul made a sobering, categorical statement: "Abstain from every form of evil" (1 Thess. 5:22). When it comes to watching media, I've found that abstinence "from every form of evil" requires me to keep my discernment alert and my remote in easy reach. What may begin as a harmless program may quickly transform into a "form of evil." How can we detect an evil entertainment form?

In *Worldly Amusements*, Wayne Wilson says that entertainment forms are evil when they either "promote an evil message" or "use evil methods."[10] Promoting an evil message is presenting sin in an appealing light. We've considered this in some detail, but it's worth noting here the nature of an evil method. Using an evil method is employing sin itself to entertain. Examples of this abound. Consider reality television programs. Commonly the sin of gossip is gratuitously thrown into the mix. Completely apart from the "game" or the "plot," participants are interviewed on a private camera in order to slander other participants. The character assassination is offered as a juicy morsel to be savored by viewers. This can seem harmless, since we don't relate with the person in real life. But the reality is that gossip is being used as an end in itself to entertain. Seemingly innocuous by cultural standards, it's an evil method using sin to entertain.

When it becomes clear that what we're watching is promoting an evil message or using an evil method, we should be proactive and stop watching. Pleasing the Lord means turning from evil in private when no one else sees or knows. The psalmist speaks of this type of integrity:

> I will walk with integrity of heart within my house; I will not set before my eyes anything that is worthless. I hate the work of those who fall away; it shall not cling to me. A perverse heart shall be far from me; I will know nothing of evil. (Ps. 101:2–4)

These verses easily apply to viewing proactively. The psalmist describes a fear of the Lord that leads him to "know nothing of evil" and to set no worthless thing before his eyes. His commitment is to "walk with integrity of heart within my house." That is, he obeys the Lord in private. If we're to similarly honor God in our homes, we must grab the remote or click the mouse when "anything that is worthless" appears.

View Accountably

Accountability is a gift to aid us in pleasing God. Thankfully, we're not called to resist the seduction of a fallen world alone. God places us in families and local churches so that we may benefit from the support of fellow believers who accompany us in our pursuit of godliness.

As I write this chapter, I've been praying for a friend who's on a business trip. Before he left, he requested that upon his return I ask him what he watched while alone in his hotel room. I respect his humility in enlisting others to stand with him in his battle with the desires of the flesh. My friend understands that defeating temptation requires exposing temptation, and so he acknowledges his battle, requests prayer, and invites inquiry regarding his viewing.

In our culture, even the church culture, television viewing usually occurs in private and is rarely discussed in public. We may speak specifically about something we saw on television, but unless we disclose our viewing habits, no one outside our family or roommates would know about the content or quantity of our TV or DVD watching. The same certainly holds true with our Internet usage. Many Christians privately explore web sites (including pornographic sites), mistakenly assuming there will be no damage to their soul and no exposure of their viewing. I believe a primary reason many Christians are either ignorant of the entertainment media's influence on their souls or powerless to change their sinful viewing practices is that their viewing remains secretive.

If we're to live in our culture's mediasphere and grow in our love for the Lord and not the world, we simply must make our media consumption a category of personal accountability, especially if we're weak in this area. It's worth asking ourselves, "Does anyone know what I watch or how much I watch?" "Have I invited anyone to ask me about my television and movie viewing?" "When I watch sinfully, do I confess my sin to anyone and ask for help?"

As you read this chapter, God may be convicting you of laziness, lust, filthy speech, pride, self-righteousness, deception, or other sins. Before you can begin to honor God with your entertainment choices, you must respond to him by acknowledging your sin, turning to the Savior, and receiving forgiveness. As you turn to Christ in repentance, turn to a brother or sister as well, asking for support and accountability. God gives grace to the humble, and as we acknowledge our need and confess our sin, we find God ready to strengthen and empower us for change. God's help often comes in the form of a fellow believer who will listen, ask questions, pray, correct, encourage, and follow up.

If you're a parent, you have the privilege and responsibility to serve and protect your family with accountability. It's wise to place televisions and computers in public areas of the home so viewing is always open to others. Another way to safeguard the family is to employ an Internet filter to block inappropriate web sites. In our part of the country, many homes are now built with media rooms that provide isolated viewing, often in a remote part of the home. Few combinations are more dangerous for a teenager than cable or satellite television, a media room, and privacy. Parents should set biblical guidelines and be aware of when, where, and what their children watch. Foolish companions are not only "out there" in the world; they can be invited into our homes if we aren't discerning about what our children view.

It's easy for parents to be passive in our supervision of the family media diet. When we've failed to exercise protective oversight for the quantity or content of our children's viewing, we should repent and ask our children's forgiveness.

Likewise, if you're a young person, you may have resisted your parents' guidelines. You may have failed to communicate honestly about web sites you've visited or your online conversations. If you've deceived your parents and secretly exposed yourself to television, films, Internet sites, or any other media that dishonors God, confess your sin and ask for your parents' forgiveness and for ongoing accountability to them.

If opening your life to others is foreign, you may see accountability as an unwelcome intrusion. I assure you it is not. Accountable viewing is a blessing and not a burden, for it positions us to experience the grace of God, the fellowship of his people, protection from sin and temptation, and the freedom of a clear conscience.

View Gratefully

Much of this chapter has appealed for deeper discernment and higher standards for television and movie watching. Given my personal and pastoral experience, it seems to me that discernment and adjustment are needed for most of us when it comes to entertainment. However, I believe we can selectively view television and film for the glory of God. I own a television and a DVD player. (Full disclosure: while making the final edits on this chapter, I've actually been shopping for a new television.) I'm not advocating cultural isolation, shunning all movies, or taking a sledgehammer to your TV set. We're free to pursue and enjoy entertainment within biblical parameters.

The Bible tells us not only what to avoid, but also what to *pursue*. Consider this pertinent passage:

> Finally, brothers, whatever is true, whatever is honorable, whatever is just, whatever is pure, whatever is lovely, whatever is commendable, if there is any excellence, if there is anything worthy of praise, think about these things. (Phil. 4:8)

Worldliness

This overarching guideline affirms rather than restricts. Messages in TV and film that correspond to these categories are valuable and may be enjoyed, even celebrated. We're not limited to watching only explicitly Christian programs or films. By God's common grace, unregenerate artists made in God's image do create works that make "true" observations about life. Unbelievers can craft "honorable" stories and "lovely" songs. They can produce films with "commendable" screenplays and "excellent" visual artistry. It's possible to enjoy entertainment media for the glory of God, and this passage helps us do so.

When we watch something true, beautiful, commendable, or excellent, our thoughts and emotions should ultimately drift heavenward. God is the source of truth, beauty, and goodness. More than that, he *is* the ultimate truth, beauty, and goodness. The discerning viewer will recognize the image of God in human art and glorify him with gratitude. For the person who has been saved by the glorious grace of God, life is to be viewed through the lens of gratitude:

> And whatever you do, in word or deed, do everything in the name of the Lord Jesus, giving thanks to God the Father through him. (Col. 3:17)

Gospel-centered living is grateful living. Whatever we do is to be done with thanks toward God. "Whatever" in this verse certainly includes entertainment. If we can't thank God with a clear conscience for a particular program or movie, we shouldn't watch it. But if we're wisely investing our time and watching something that's true, honorable, just, pure, lovely, commendable, excellent, or praiseworthy (Phil. 4:8), then by all means we should thank God for it. We shouldn't watch sheepishly or with a vague sense of guilt, but freely thanking God for the viewing experience. God is honored not only by our avoiding sin but also by our active gratitude for the many good things he provides, including drama, cinematography, creativity, beauty, and laughter.

To be clear: we *can* watch television or go to the movies and glorify God by it. To do so, we must be motivated by grace, and we must view selectively, proactively, accountably, and gratefully.

While I'm optimistic about the possibility of watching for the glory of God, I'm also realistic about life in the mediasphere. For most of us, applying biblical discernment and viewing with discretion will mean watching less than we currently do. But that's no great loss. It means more time to interact with actual people—a date with your spouse, talk-time or play-time with your children, fellowship with your friends, serving people in your church, or reaching out to unbelievers. There's a world of things to do with the TV turned off.

Many of us could use a vacation from viewing, some rest and relaxation from the constant distraction of entertainment media. Dropping the remote and getting off the sofa won't guarantee we'll escape worldly drift, but it's a step in the right direction. And each step counts when we're resisting the seduction of a fallen world.

Will you take the first step now?

Chapter Three

God, My Heart, and Music

Bob Kauflin

IN TWENTY-FIRST-CENTURY AMERICA, we love our music. Satellite radio, CDs, streaming Internet, and iPods enable us to live our lives to a constant soundtrack. Walk through any public venue and you'll see dozens of people oblivious to their surroundings, tuned in to whatever's pouring through their ear buds. For many of us, life without music would be unthinkable, undesirable, and unbearable.

But we don't always have the choice to forgo music. There are times I've felt like I couldn't escape it even if I wanted to. We're subjected to music in grocery stores, elevators, doctor's offices, shopping malls, coffee shops, theme parks, restaurants, and every public setting imaginable. It's not just the hills that are alive with the sound of music. It's our entire culture.

Do you ever think about the effect all this music might be having on us? On you? Is it all just innocent entertainment? Can we listen to too much music? Could there be consequences we're completely unaware of?

As a professional musician for the past thirty years, and someone who has over forty days of music on my iTunes,

I've asked myself these questions more than once. It only makes sense to find out if so much music is a good thing or a bad thing. And if you're a Christian who listens to or makes music in today's culture, you should be asking yourself these questions as well.

To find some answers, we need to look beyond the current music climate. We need to start at the beginning.

God's Idea

Music is God's idea, and apparently he enjoys it immensely. He told King David, "a man after his own heart," to schedule musicians who would play and sing regularly before his presence at the tabernacle (1 Sam. 13:14; 1 Chron. 16:5–7). The psalms regularly exhort us to sing a new song to the Lord and to praise him to the sound of musical instruments (Ps. 33:1; 150). Jesus sang with his disciples (Matt. 26:30), and we're told to speak to one another "in psalms and hymns and spiritual songs" (Eph. 5:19). And music isn't just for this life. The book of Revelation tells us that music will continue into eternity, where we'll forever sing the praises of the Lamb who was slain.

But God's intentions for music include more than public worship settings. In the Bible, music also accompanies war, work, funerals, love, and play (Ex. 32:17–18; Isa. 16:10; Matt. 11:17; Judg. 11:34; Isa. 5:1; Matt. 11:17). God created us to enjoy both making and listening to music. Musical activities have been an everyday part of life for thousands of years, enabling us to express more deeply our joys, our sorrows, and a hundred other aspects of the human condition.

With the variety of music styles in the world, I've sometimes wondered if God has a favorite kind of music. Does he like folk more than jazz? Classical more than hard rock? Does he prefer the lilting sound of flutes to the blaring of bagpipes? Occasionally I have this fear that we'll get to heaven and find out that God's favorite music is opera.

Actually, it seems that God likes music of all kinds. No one style can sufficiently capture his glory or even begin to reflect the vastness of his wisdom, creativity, beauty, and order. That doesn't mean some kinds of music aren't more complex or beautiful than others. It just means no single genre of music is better than the rest in every way. As Harold Best puts it:

> God is not Western; God is not Eastern; God is not exclusively the God of classical culture or of primitive culture; God is the Lord of the plethora, the God of the diverse, the redeemer of the plural. . . . Pentecost tells us that one artistic tongue is only a start and a thousand will never suffice. There is no single chosen language or artistic or musical style that, better than all others, can capture and repeat back the fullness of the glory of God.[1]

So what does music have to do with worldliness, the focus of this book?

To answer that question, we have to ask a few more. What motivates us to like the music we do? Is music entirely neutral? Why does music affect us so deeply? Does the music I listen to affect my thoughts or behavior in any way? Does it say anything about my relationship with God? Most important, are my music choices consistent with the gospel that has saved me?

If these questions don't seem important, think again. Music can be more dangerous than most of us realize. It has the potential to harden our hearts and weaken our faith. In fact, a wise Christian understands that *listening to music without discernment and godly intent reveals a heart willing to flirt with the world.*

Without discernment we won't be alert to the effects music might be having on us. Without godly intent we'll be listening to it for the wrong reasons. We'll be failing to fulfill the purpose for which Christ redeemed us. Paul tells us, "You are not your own, for you were bought with a price. So glorify God in your body" (1 Cor. 6:19–20). We were ransomed from hell so we could glorify God.

Music is one more way God intends for us to do that.

It's Just Music—or Is It?

Music can be simply defined as an organized combination of melody, harmony, and rhythm. For non-musicians, melody is the part you can whistle, harmony describes the music that supports the melody, and rhythm is the beat.

Those three elements in themselves carry no moral value. There are no "evil" melodies or "false" rhythms. Music alone is incapable of lying to us or commanding us to do wrong. Music by itself is also unable to communicate "truth statements" to us. A melody can't unpack the meaning of Christ's substitutionary atonement, a chord progression can't clearly articulate that God created the world, and no beat can express the meaning of the incarnation.

But music affects our emotions in profound ways. Some say it's related to the effect music has on our body chemistry. One journalist noted that "physiological links between melody and the mind are far greater than we ever imagined," and that "listening to and playing music actually can alter how our brains and . . . our bodies function." His comments concluded with a quote from opera star Denyce Graves: "Whether or not people choose to recognize the power of music, it remains a spiritual experience, a healing experience. It can save us."[2]

No, music *can't* save us. But it can deeply affect us.

The passions music draws out range from noble to base, from simple to complex, from God-glorifying to sensual. That's why people who write advertising jingles, pop songs, and film scores can make a decent living. They know music speaks powerfully to our emotions. Most of us are touched by the music we hear, even when we're unaware of it. In fact, sometimes we realize how music is affecting us only when we notice it's not playing anymore.

So why *does* music affect us? Often our responses are based on learned musical principles. To most Americans, fast music in a major key sounds happy, while slow music in a minor key signifies sadness. When those signals are mixed, we tend to get disoriented. If someone plays "Here Comes the Bride" in a minor key or *The 1812 Overture* at half the normal speed, even non-musicians will inherently know something's wrong. They may not be able to describe it in musical terms, but they'll know the song isn't communicating what it's supposed to. Musical principles are being violated.

Attentiveness can also determine the way music influences us. If I'm engaged in deep conversation with my wife at Starbucks, I'm not always aware of the music being pumped through the speakers. It's a different story when I'm at home reviewing a newly purchased CD or listening to it repeatedly on my iPod. Music tends to move us more if our minds are focused on it.

There are other reasons music affects us, such as volume, familiarity, and our background. But probably no aspect of music affects us more than the things we associate with it.

A few years ago, members of my family endured repeated cases of strep throat. As one person recovered, someone else fell ill. We finally found out why. My oldest son was a "carrier," never getting sick himself but continually passing on the bacteria to others.

Music is like my son—a carrier. Because music can't be handled, smelled, or seen, it tends to get its meaning from the things that surround it. Sometimes those associations are positive, like a song from your wedding or carols on Christmas Eve. But sometimes we associate music with negative, even sinful, things. And if we don't realize what music is "carrying," worldly attitudes and desires can influence and affect our unsuspecting hearts.

I've found music can be a carrier of at least three elements: content, context, and culture.

Music Conveys Content

The most obvious connection we make with music is content, meaning the lyrics. In the previous chapter, Craig Cabaniss pointed out how Philippians 4:8 should guide our media choices. That same verse provides God's standards for content in the songs we listen to. It tells us what music should lead us to think about.

> Finally, brothers, whatever is true, whatever is honorable, whatever is just, whatever is pure, whatever is lovely, whatever is commendable, if there is any excellence, if there is anything worthy of praise, think about these things. (Phil. 4:8)

These biblical standards instantly bring into question much of the music that's currently popular and available to us. When I don't even consider ungodly lyrical content in the songs I listen to, I'm allowing music to seduce me.

It's not uncommon for Christians on Sunday mornings to worship Jesus for his substitutionary death on the cross, then sing songs during the week that exalt the sins he died for. We sing, "My chains are gone, I've been set free," then remain enslaved to lyrics that promote fornication, profanity, anger, godless pleasure, sensuality, and materialism. "From the same mouth come blessing and cursing. My brothers, these things ought not to be so" (James 3:10). James is right. These things ought not to be so. But when someone expresses a concern about song lyrics, we usually have a ready reply: "I don't even listen to the words. I don't know what they're saying."

My response is, "Why not?" Christians, of all people, should be asking what songs actually mean. We're to "do all to the glory of God" (1 Cor. 10:31). And if we "never" listen to the words attached to music, we're training ourselves to tune out the content of songs and simply allow the music to affect us. That makes it all the more difficult to focus on the truths we sing on Sundays. We'll tend to be more influenced by the sound, beat, and tempo than the word of Christ we're proclaiming.

Don't misunderstand me. Listening to a song with sexually suggestive lyrics won't cause you to run to the Internet and start downloading pornography. Hearing a song with profanity doesn't mean you'll be peppering your conversations tomorrow with four-letter words. But over time the lyrics to songs can weaken our defenses, blur our discernment, and redirect our affections toward the world. Listening to music is never neutral, because our sinful hearts are involved.

Drift won't happen right away. And you probably won't even notice it. One of my unmarried daughters confessed to me how listening to "harmless" romantic songs for a season had contributed toward her general lack of spiritual passion. Another young woman's descent into immorality began with repeated exposure to music that glamorized rebellion and idolized love based on sexual attraction. I've known guys who work out to songs with angry, profane lyrics because they say the music motivates them to push themselves harder. One day they find themselves singing along to words they used to tune out, words they would be embarrassed to repeat in the presence of their parents or a pastor.

Music with ungodly lyrics can persuade us to love things we wouldn't ordinarily love—specifically the "desires of the flesh and the desires of the eyes and pride in possessions" (1 John 2:16). I've seen it happen in my children, in my friends, and in my own life. It can happen in you. We're foolish to repeatedly subject ourselves to songs whose lyrics could dull our conscience and make us glory in sinful desires rather than the cross of Christ (Gal. 6:14).

Sometimes we pride ourselves in what we can handle, as if exposing ourselves to temptation were a virtue. That attitude reminds me of a story I once read about a group of coach drivers applying for a job. One of them would be chosen to carry the king's children up and down a narrow, winding road leading up to the king's mountain-top castle. With dozens of steep drop-offs and no guardrails, it was a daunting assignment.

The king's chief liveryman asked each candidate this question: "How close can you get to the edge without going over?"

The applicants offered various responses indicating their confidence and skill. One man boasted he could drive the horses at nearly full speed for the entire length of the road, always keeping within six inches from the edge.

The interviewer was unimpressed. Finally, one driver stepped forward and responded, "Sir, if it's the king's children, I want to stay as far from the edge as I possibly can."

He was hired.

If we're concerned about the seductive effect worldly lyrics can have on our souls, we won't be racing close to the edge of sin, seeing how much we can take in before it finally starts affecting us. We won't be tempting ourselves with music that contains profanity, sensuality, rebellion, or other worldly attitudes. We'll want to stay as far from the edge as we can.

Music Conveys Context

A second element music carries is context. Context refers to the environments we connect with music—the places, events, and people that surround the music we listen to on a regular basis.

There are two aspects to this. One is the past contexts that listening to music evokes. A traditional hymn might signify profound devotion to someone who grew up in a God-honoring church but lifeless formalism to a person whose upbringing was nominally Christian. Our feelings about a particular song or musical style can be significantly influenced by the contexts we've heard it in.

Harold Best relates the true story of a young man who became involved in a satanic cult that used a certain type of music in its rituals. Eventually the young man became a Christian. A few months after his conversion, he was sitting in a church service when fear suddenly gripped his heart. The organist was playing music that reminded him of the satanic cult he'd left. In confusion, he fled the building. The music he heard happened to be written by Johann Sebastian Bach, a devout Christian acknowledged by many as one of the greatest composers in history. But the young man found it difficult to separate the music he heard from its original evil context.[3]

Another way to think about context is the environments in which we listen to music currently. Your contexts for enjoying music probably aren't directly tied to the worship of demons, but they might be no less dangerous. If you attend concerts or events where the artists or the crowd intentionally promote sensuality, godlessness, or rebellion, you're flirting with the world. And you might not even be aware of it.

I've known young people, raised by Christian parents, who at some point became attracted to a particular music group or style. To fulfill their musical appetite, they started to frequent clubs, bars, and concerts. They sought out ungodly friends who shared the same musical preferences, oblivious to the potential effect on their souls. They started watching music videos that exploited sexuality. When their parents challenged them, they responded, "I just like the music." But over time their wardrobe, mannerisms, and attitudes changed to reflect their new influences. Some of them walked away from the faith. Music had become the carrier of the worldly contexts that surrounded it.

Radio is another context in which we can listen to music. Some Christians regularly tune in to secular radio shows. There's nothing inherently wrong with that. We read books written by non-Christians, watch movies produced by non-Christians, and certainly can enjoy certain songs written by non-Christians. However, along with the questionable content of many songs, DJ's often make comments that reflect the world's attitudes toward sex, relationships, use of language, and life in general.

My non-Christian neighbor once told me he wouldn't listen to his normal radio station when his six-year-old son was in the car because the announcer's chatter between songs was so offensive. He didn't see the glaring contradiction in his life. Unfortunately, many Christians aren't any more discerning.

Where I hear my music makes a difference.

Music Conveys Culture

A third element music can reflect is culture.

Culture describes the *values* we connect with music. It's how we respond to, shape, organize, and rule our surroundings. Culture changes from generation to generation, from nation to nation, and from family to family. That's why we can enjoy some songs now that might have been labeled "evil" back in the '50s or '60s because of the beat, the musicians' long hair, or the psychedelic colors on the album covers. Many of those songs are now connected to a movie, a commercial, or a product rather than a rebellious generation. What they "mean" has changed along with their cultural associations.

Culture isn't the same as worldliness. Our society's cultural makeup has both positive and negative characteristics. We can seek to relate to our culture without being worldly. But worldliness—self-exalting opposition to God—is present in every culture and can be found in anything associated with the music we listen to: packaging, advertisements, pictures, and web sites, as well as a musical artist's clothing, attitudes, and interviews.

Many of the songs at the top of the charts are filled with ungodly aspects of our culture, stemming from the lives of those who make and market the music. See if you can recognize any of them in your favorite music:

- independence and rebellion ("I am my own authority");
- emotionalism ("To feel is to know");
- temporal narcissism ("Five years ago is ancient history");
- love of pleasure ("It's all about me");
- sexual immorality ("Marriage and purity are so *yesterday*");
- transience ("Eat, drink, and be merry, for tomorrow we die").

You might not intentionally and enthusiastically embrace any of these values. But all of them can find their way into our hearts through the music we enjoy.

It's important to note that music and its associations don't create sin in our hearts—they simply reveal what's already there. If I chafe at my parents' authority, I'm going to be drawn to friends and contexts that allow me to express my independence. If I'm intent on feeding my appetite for sensual pleasures, I can easily justify watching music videos, even though I'll be regularly confronted with sexually provocative images. If I'm given to self-pity ("Why doesn't anyone recognize how good/important/special I am?"), I'll be drawn to music that's melancholic, depressing, and hopeless. If I value what I feel over what I know to be true, I'll tend to listen to music that feels good rather than music that's good for me.

God tells us in Galatians 1:4 that Jesus "gave himself for our sins to deliver us from *the present evil age,* according to the will of our God and Father." Jesus died on the cross to deliver us from the penalty of our sins *and* from the world's attitudes and desires. We've been set free from its destructive and deceptive grip. The "present evil age" doesn't refer to a specific type of music, a certain artist, or a particular decade. It's much broader than that. It's an underlying anti-God approach to all of life. And it can be found in the music we listen to.

At this point, maybe you'd like me to suggest a list of artists or music styles that every Christian should either pursue or avoid. Sorry, but that list doesn't exist. And if it did, I'm not convinced it would be helpful. What's appropriate for one person to listen to might be sin for someone else because of the differing associations we make. We rarely hear music in a vacuum. Depending on the state of our hearts, any song we hear is a potential carrier of worldly values and perspectives.

Rather than a list, I offer you two questions.

First, does the music you listen to lead you to love the Savior more or cause your affections for Christ to diminish?

Second, does your music lead you to value an eternal perspective or influence you to adopt the mindset of this "present evil age"?

Answering these questions honestly is an important step toward making wise decisions about the music you listen to and living a life worthy of the gospel.

The Effect of Ignorance: Compromise

If we don't take the time to soberly evaluate our music listening habits, we can become oblivious to the worldly propaganda music carries. We can be led into compromise. Here are some of the signs that you're already there.

You seldom or never use Scripture to evaluate your decisions about music. Hopefully, you've seen by now that while Scripture may not address specific styles of music, it does address the hearts that are listening. We may assume God gave us music just to make us happy, not holy; he actually gave us music to make us happy *and* holy.

Music is far too significant a part of our lives for us to assume it won't affect us. Proverbs 14:15 reminds us, "The simple believes everything, but the prudent gives thought to his steps." Discernment in music is simply one part of the overall discernment we're called to exercise as disciples of Jesus Christ. Unexamined listening habits leave us at the mercy of our own sinful desires and the influence of a godless culture.

Another area Scripture addresses is how our music listening affects those around us. Jesus strongly warned those who caused little ones to sin (Luke 17:1–2). Does your music provide a temptation for new Christians, younger siblings, children, and non-discerning peers? How are you demonstrating love to others through the music you're exposing them to?

Your music listening is characterized by objectionable content or ungodly contexts. "Whoever walks with the wise becomes wise, but the companion of fools will suffer harm" (Prov. 13:20). The music we listen to regularly becomes a "companion" that informs our view of the world, influences our emotional state, and affects our thinking. If we wouldn't trust a non-Christian to give us counsel on how to live our lives, why would we regularly listen to their counsel set to music?

Christians often justify their questionable music choices by saying that music produced by non-Christians is more creative than Christian music. They praise artists like the Red Hot Chili Peppers, Dave Matthews Band, Jay-Z, and others for their musical innovation and originality. There's no doubt they're creative. What we can forget is that non-Christian companies and bands are also more creative in deceiving us to love the world. They aren't trying to care for our souls; they want us to buy their product. They want us to forget there's a God to whom we're accountable for our every word, thought, and action. If you consistently choose ungodly music as your companion, you won't be the exception. You too will suffer harm.

There are numerous ways we can look for creative music that won't require subjecting ourselves to the world's mind-set and values. I've scanned radio stations, used web sites like Pandora.com, listened to 30-second clips on iTunes, or followed up on recommendations from friends.

But in the end, seeking out and listening to "creative" music isn't a right we can demand at the expense of biblical standards. It could be a sign that we're worshiping at the altar of innovation rather than at the foot of the cross.

Your priorities and schedule revolve around music. A friend confessed to me once that he turned on the radio every time he entered his bedroom, regardless of how long he planned to be there. He began to realize that being able to listen to music "whenever he wanted" was becoming a form of bondage, not freedom. Another friend told me he had difficulty living without the MP3 file-sharing service he had access to in college. He was bothered by the fact that he could no longer keep up with and buy the newest music. As he considered a music subscription service, he started to question how much time he'd have to commit to exploring unlimited downloads. He wisely decided against it.

The fact that new music exists doesn't mean I have to own it. Often, our obsession with music leaves less time for activities with more eternal value—Bible study, prayer, personal reflection, and serving others.

How much time do you spend looking for music to download? Browsing through CDs at Borders? Talking to friends about music, or singing lyrics in your head?

Burning CDs? Watching music videos? Scanning iTunes? What does the time you invest say about the hold music might have on you? If you're easily irritated when you aren't hearing the music you prefer, or if you're more passionate about a concert than participation in your church, music is more than a hobby. It's an idol.

Your passion for Christ has waned; your passion for music hasn't. There can be many explanations for our diminished zeal for God. Sometimes the most obvious reason is that we're feasting regularly at the world's table of delights. I've watched Christians dramatically encounter God and then gradually revert to sinful patterns because they failed to change their music listening habits. Sadly and predictably, they were seduced by the world's empty promises communicated through the music they listened to.

In his letter to the Philippians, Paul grieves over those who "glory in their shame, with minds set on earthly things" (Phil. 3:19). He describes them as "enemies of the cross of Christ" (3:18). When the music we regularly listen to glories in what should shame us and directs our minds to earthly things, we're being more than unwise. We're exposing ourselves to a message associated with the enemies of the cross—the cross that purchased our forgiveness and freed us from the bondage of our sinful desires.

Using Music for God's Glory

We've spent most of this chapter focusing on the ways music can be a carrier of worldly attitudes and perspectives. But that's not the end of the story. Music is meant to be a means of bringing glory to God, one more way in which we can "proclaim the excellencies of him who called [us] out of darkness into his marvelous light" (1 Pet. 2:9). I want to suggest specific steps to help us use music in a way that benefits our souls and honors the Savior.

Evaluate your current intake of music. If you've read this far and thought, "I don't need to evaluate the quality or quantity of my music," you're probably wrong. Because indwelling sin is so deceptive, I usually have a difficult time seeing the effect music is having on me. Areas to consider include how much music you listen to, what types, in what situations and times of day, and for how long. Ask your friends, parents, or a pastor to get their perspective on whether your music listening is characterized by biblical discernment and a desire to please God. Make sure they give you an honest answer. It could be the means God uses to deliver you from the world's grasp.

Delete or throw away music you'll listen to only if you backslide. When we become Christians, God transforms our hearts. We're no longer those who live "in the passions of our flesh, carrying out the desires of the body and the mind" (Eph. 2:3). Pursuits we once found appealing no longer interest us and at times even repulse us. But more often than not, music that might tempt us stays on our computers, in our CD collection, or on our MP3 player. Whether the reason is negligence, lack of time, or the thought that we might find it appealing at a later date, it's wise to get rid of what could hinder our growth in Christ.

Listen to music with others. As my children were growing up, we had one CD player in the house that served as the family listening center. Music was a family activity and no one developed his or her own private listening habits. Those days are long gone. But listening to music with others is still a good idea. Part of the joy music communicates comes from sharing it. If you only listen to music through a set of headphones, consider investing in a set of speakers for your iPod or an audio system for your home. And don't insist on listening to music only *you* like.

Make music rather than listen to it. You don't have to be especially gifted to play a guitar or plunk out chords on a piano. But even if you don't play an instrument, you can obey God's command to sing (Ps. 47:6). Producing music ourselves frees us from thinking that the joy music provides depends on technology.

Go on a music fast. At American University, students in a class called "Understanding Mass Media" were shocked to learn mid-semester that the course requirements included a 24-hour media fast: "No television, computers, iPods or other MP3 devices, radio, video games, CD players, records, or cell phones (or land lines) for 24 hours." One student described it as "grueling pain"; another called it "one of the toughest days I have had to endure."[4] But everyone lived to tell about it, and some even thought they benefited from the assignment.

Maybe you can't imagine giving up your music for a month, a week, or even a day. But there are few more effective ways to measure the place music holds in your life, thinking, and behavior. It doesn't even have to be a full fast. You can try driving in silence for twenty minutes rather than listening to the radio or your iPod. You can establish a limit to how much music you listen to each day.

Whatever kind of fast you choose, it's sure to leave you with more time to pray, read your Bible, and serve others.

Keep track of how much music you buy. Rhapsody, iTunes, and other downloading services have made it easier to lose track of how much you're actually spending on music. Before you know it, you've racked up one hundred dollars in charges for music you "had" to have. Realistically, some of us can't even listen to all the music we buy. Figure out a budget for what you should be spending and stick to it.

Broaden your musical tastes. Music is neither a demon to be feared nor a god to be idolized. It's simply a part of God's creation intended to serve his glory and our good. That means we can appreciate a wide variety of different styles and expressions of music. But when it comes to music, most of us know what we like and like what we know. We rarely venture out into new styles and genres. In fact, we excel at mocking the tastes of those we think are less musically informed—people who like country, opera, or pop, for instance. Try asking your friends with different musical tastes to suggest songs or albums you should listen to. Discover what they enjoy about a particular style or artist and what aspect of God's glory you might be missing by not listening to it.

Listen to old music. Human beings have been making music at least since the fourth chapter of Genesis, where we're told that Jubal "was the father of all those who play the lyre and pipe" (Gen. 4:21). A lot of music has been written, sung, and recorded since then. And yet we can still think the best music is what was produced in the past ten years—or worse, what's coming out next month. Music that stands the test of time is worth giving our attention to. That doesn't mean everything written in the past is great music. But we're shortsighted, proud, and poorer if we never appreciate the music God has given us throughout history.

Intentionally thank God every time you enjoy music. Music is a gift from God. But God never intends his gifts to replace him as the object of our desire and delight. Music may be able to calm our hurried spirits, encourage our troubled hearts, and strengthen our weary souls—but not like our Savior can. He has redeemed us by his death, sympathizes with us in our weaknesses, and is able to give us mercy and grace in our time of need (Eph. 1:7; Heb. 4:15–16). Music, like all of God's gifts, is meant to draw our hearts and attention to his glory, his power, and his love.

We can use music to deepen our love for God in countless ways. The most obvious way is proclaiming God's truth together in corporate worship, pouring out our hearts to him in song, encountering his presence. Some people find it helpful to sing with or listen to a worship CD during their private devotions. But as we've seen, God isn't concerned only about music in "religious" settings. He intends us to use music for his glory everywhere. As we listen to a skilled jazz guitarist or a concert pianist, we can thank God for his gifts of creativity, talent, sound, and beauty. A new mother singing a lullaby can reflect on God's tenderness and mercy. Playing CDs on different occasions can provide moving accompaniment that heightens the significance of important moments and relationships.

Ultimately, music is a means of deepening our love for and enjoyment of the One who gave us this gift in the first place. In *The Weight of Glory*, C. S. Lewis expressed it like this:

The books or the music in which we thought the beauty was located will betray us if we trust to them. . . . For they are not the thing itself; they are only the scent of a flower we have not found, the echo of a tune we have not heard, news from a country we have never yet visited.[5]

No music, however beautiful, however impressive, however technologically creative or emotionally moving, can rival the wonder and breathtaking beauty of the Savior, who came as a man to live a perfect life and die an atoning death in our place.

Giving up, reducing, or changing your music diet may feel like a sacrifice. It just might be. You may have to sacrifice looking cool to your friends to please your heavenly Father. You might have to sacrifice slavery to earthly appetites and pleasures so you can pursue and enjoy eternal ones. (Can we even call those sacrifices?)

But no sacrifice we make compares to the ultimate sacrifice of Jesus Christ. He redeemed us to purchase our forgiveness and to earn us a place among those who "no longer live for themselves but for him who for their sake died and was raised" (2 Cor. 5:15).

That means music is no longer ours to use however we want. It never was. It was never meant to provide what can be found only in a relationship with the Savior.

Music is a precious gift, but it makes a terrible god.

By God's grace, may we always know the difference.

Chapter Four

God, My Heart, and Stuff

Dave Harvey

IT REALLY HAD NO special meaning for me. Except that in seeing it, I noticed it was *mine*.

I arrived home late to a party that was well under way. Upon entering, I spotted him—my brother-in-law. Wearing *my* sweatshirt—my "I'm-home-ready-to-relax-and-rule-my-domain" sweatshirt.

Oblivious to the crowd mingling around my house, I determined to explore this breach of protocol. Spotting my wife carrying two trays of hors d'oeuvres, I took the subtle approach. "Why is he wearing my sweatshirt? Is he going to give it back? Who died and made him Dave?" For some reason, she was unmoved by the injustice of it all.

But it was my sweatshirt, and I needed an answer—immediately!

In Scripture, we find Jesus' response to someone else in the throes of "mine." But it was no party. And the stakes were higher than a sweatshirt.

Ask a Dumb Question . . .

The crowd was vast. "So many thousands of the people had gathered together," Luke tells us, "that they were trampling one another" (Luke 12:1). They were witnessing a conflict, with battle lines clearly drawn.

On one side: Jesus Christ—a messiah to some, a rebel to others.

On the other: the Pharisees, the religious establishment of that day.

Words flew as the rift widened between the prophet and the religious elite. The skirmish intensified when Jesus openly challenged the Pharisees. "You fools!" he exclaimed as he exposed their hypocrisy in detail. "Woe to you Pharisees! . . . Woe to you!" (11:39–44).

They, in turn, took aim. "The scribes and the Pharisees began to press him hard and to provoke him to speak about many things, *lying in wait for him, to catch him in something he might say*" (11:53–54).

It was a turf war for the hearts of men. There would be no surrender, no negotiation. Only an inevitable showdown.

In this context, and while the crowds in the background pressed in, Jesus turned to his disciples and said, "Beware of the leaven of the Pharisees, which is hypocrisy" (12:1). He went on to instruct them further, the people pressing closer to hear his words. Suddenly a man from the vast crowd interrupted.

As he spoke up, many in the crowd must have wondered, "Who is he? Does he seek a wise saying from the Great Teacher? Some blessing perhaps? Maybe a divine healing?"

Worldliness

"Teacher," the man said, "tell my brother to divide the inheritance with me" (Luke 12:13).

Talk about missing your cue!

But let's reset the stage. Who's being addressed here? Jesus has just told them who he is—the Son of Man[1] (12:8, 10), the One who stands as reconciler between the Holy God and sinful man, the deliverer out of bondage, and the One who will reign over all. No one can claim this title but the Messiah—and everybody present knows it!

Except, apparently, one guy. What could be so urgent that he would air his family's dirty laundry *right now*? If you're going to interrupt the Son of Man, shouldn't you at least request something significant? Maybe a sign or wonder? A miracle perhaps?

And yet, more surprising than the man's intrusion is the response of Christ.

As readers of the Gospel accounts, you and I know that when Jesus takes note of individuals in the crowd—particularly if they're approaching with a concern about other people's sin—they become the next object lesson. So let's watch and listen.

"Take care, and be on your guard against all covetousness, for one's life does not consist in the abundance of his possessions" (12:15).

That's the biblical equivalent of a flag on the field. It's meant to stop the action. The Greek word translated here as "take care" is an imperative, present, active verb carrying considerable force for a warning. Some versions translate it, "Beware!"

Now, before we align with Team Jesus and root him on,

let's remember that we're more similar to Mr. Oblivious than we might like to believe. In fact, it seems the reason Jesus is singling this guy out is for the benefit of us all. Jesus stood in this crowd for this very reason—to reveal the truth and worth of God. The Son of Man is to be cherished above all because he came to reconcile sinners to God through his atoning sacrifice, to deliver us out of bondage into eternal life with him, and to display his glorious reign through a people of his own possession. To value him and celebrate his worth is not just important, it's the whole point.

So, back to *beware*. Beware of what?

Well, first the good news: the guy's problem was not his brother. But that led to bad news: the guy's problem was himself! Christ taught that this man's greatest problem was not his brother's selfishness but the materialism in his own soul. Yet this is no mere prophet simply denouncing sin; this is the Son of Man on a rescue mission.

Let's take time to understand why the rescue is necessary.

Getting to the Heart of Materialism

Oil tycoon J. Paul Getty once said, "The best things in life ... are things."[2] This is the mantra of materialism.

Materialism is fundamentally a focus on and a trust in what we can touch and possess. It describes the unchecked desire for, dependence on, and stockpiling of *stuff*. In some people it's more painfully obvious than in others. But it pervades every heart.

Materialism is a far deeper problem than having stuff. It's an expression of worldliness with incredibly persuasive force.

Worldliness

One journalist described the profound sway of consumerism (a current synonym for materialism) in these terms:

> Consumerism was the triumphant winner of the ideological wars of the 20th century, beating out both religion and politics as the path millions of Americans follow to find purpose, meaning, order and transcendent exaltation in their lives. Liberty in this market democracy has, for many, come to mean freedom to buy as much as you can of whatever you wish, endlessly reinventing and telegraphing your sense of self with each new purchase.[3]

That observation confirms the persistent ignorance or rejection still today of the point Jesus made: "One's life does not consist in the abundance of his possessions."

We have an inescapable tendency to link who we are with what we have. It's what Jesus rescued us from, what consumerism produces in us, and what J. Paul Getty relished. When Jesus reminds us that life doesn't consist in the abundance of possessions, this isn't just a truism. It's a teaching moment, because in essence materialism is a problem in the human heart.

In exposing materialism, the real issue for Christ is not the stuff around us but the stuff within. The Savior loves us so much that he comes after our coveting hearts and rescues us from the seduction of a fallen world.

Coveting is an awkward word. It seems outdated, Victorian-like. Even the whisper of it conjures ominous images of Puritans and prophets and the Ten Commandments and "for goodness' sake, leave your neighbors' stuff alone!" What is covetousness, anyway? How do we know when we're coveting?

Simply stated, coveting is *desiring stuff too much* or *desiring too much stuff.* It's replacing our delight in God with joy in stuff. Materialism is what happens when coveting has cash to spend.

In itself, stuff isn't bad. In fact, if received with gratitude, used in moderation, and stewarded in faith, stuff can be a tremendous resource for God's purposes. In eighteenth-century England, the Countess of Huntingdon, one of the richest women in the British Empire, used her wealth and properties to further the evangelical revival of that day. Her homes became strategic meeting places for men like George Whitefield. Her possessions were constantly at the disposal of her Lord. Her vision of God moved her sight beyond stuff.

But covetousness is a glutton for stuff. Through covetous attractions and distractions within the heart, our stuff takes on meaning in our lives far beyond what God intends. In fact, the apostle Paul makes the point that covetousness is a form of idol worship (Eph. 5:5; Col. 3:5). Idolatrous cravings maneuver our hearts away from God and affix them to things of this world. Hence the ultimatum from Jesus recorded for us later in Luke:

> No servant can serve two masters, for either he will hate the one and love the other, or he will be devoted to the one and despise the other. You cannot serve God and money. (Luke 16:13)

Covetousness is choosing earthly trinkets over eternal treasure.

Worldliness

The sin of covetousness is not that we have stuff; it's that *our stuff has us*. That's why, when that man in the crowd interrupted Jesus, he found it so easy to ignore what the Master was teaching and to demand a ruling on his belongings. Covetousness blinded him from everything but his momentary object of worship—a family inheritance. The irony is that he was face-to-face with the only One truly worthy of worship, yet all he could see was what he lacked. He had stuff on his mind and wrapped around his heart.

Coveting is an equal-opportunity sin. It stalks the rich and poor alike. The audience gathered around the Lord that day consisted largely of peasants, yet Christ took aim at their coveting and unbelief by relating the parable of the rich fool (12:13–21). The issue is not tax brackets; it's desires.

Consider the following true story:

> Many years ago a major American company had trouble keeping employees working in their assembly plant in Panama. The laborers lived in a generally agrarian, barter economy, but the company paid them in cash. Since the average employee had more cash after a week's work than he had ever seen, he would periodically quit working, satisfied with what he had made. What was the solution? Company executives gave all their employees a Sears catalog. No one quit then, because they all wanted the previously undreamed-of things they saw in that book.[4]

The lesson is clear. The mere availability of stuff can ignite covetous desires. But we're called to walk a different road. As this book's title suggests—*Worldliness: Resisting the*

Seduction of a Fallen World—we're to battle covetousness at the level of our desires.

In my travels, I've visited believers living in poverty in the Philippines, Ghana, South Africa, India, and Sri Lanka. It's utterly inspiring to see courageous Christians endure and prevail in surroundings of squalor. The Western church has much to learn about suffering from poor Christians in the world. But the temptation to covet can be just as strong whether the stuff in question is a neighbor's goat or a neighbor's golf clubs.

Yes, affluence can be a spiritual disability that dulls people to their need for God. Jesus was quite serious in saying, "How difficult it is for those who have wealth to enter the kingdom of God!" (Luke 18:24). But this doesn't mean God is biased against the rich; it means the rich are often biased against God. Their affluence feels like it meets needs, but it really diverts attention from the Savior to their stuff.

Locating materialism and consumerism in the coveting heart is important. It offers a biblical diagnosis for a common social malady. Consumer ailments don't begin with shopping addictions or "an offer I couldn't refuse." The real problem is sin. Austerity and indulgence won't cure the bankruptcy of soul and emptiness of life that commonly result when our covetous desires are allowed free reign.

Just as Jesus stood before the man in Luke 12, God's remedy for sin stands in the person of Jesus Christ. This Jesus was and is poised to liberate, seeking to unshackle the covetous heart with a vision of freedom secured at the cross. Covetousness may be powerful, but it's no match for a benevolent Savior.

Trapped by Something We Don't Even See

But to appreciate God's solution, one must understand man's problem. So Jesus illustrates the dangers of a covetous heart:

> The land of a rich man produced plentifully, and he thought to himself, "What shall I do, for I have nowhere to store my crops?" And he said, "I will do this: I will tear down my barns and build larger ones, and there I will store all my grain and my goods. And I will say to my soul, Soul, you have ample goods laid up for many years; relax, eat, drink, be merry." But God said to him, "Fool! This night your soul is required of you, and the things you have prepared, whose will they be?" So is the one who lays up treasure for himself and is not rich toward God. (Luke 12:16–21)

It's a simple tale with two brief parts, two characters. Enter the rich man. He's thinking, "Business is good, and it's time to consider storage upgrades." Needing strategic advice to form a business plan, he calls upon the most trusted consultant he knows—himself. Building bigger barns is the reasonable plan he devises for stewarding his increased resources. Inspired by his own genius, he comforts his soul, satisfied that he's invested wisely and earned a little time off.

Enter the Divine Auditor—and a shocking discovery. The rich man's number has come up, and it's time for the great accounting of his investments in heaven. In the only audit that truly matters, the rich man's portfolio is bare! The stuff he's acquired in life will go to another. Facing eternity, he stands bankrupt with nothing to show but debts he cannot pay. All he has now is a new name: Fool.

What's the moral of the story? I believe it's simply this: *covetousness chains the heart to things that are passing away*.

Take a look around you. Every object you see is confined to this world. And in the end, every treasured possession remains behind.

On November 26, 1922, Howard Carter made archaeological history by unearthing the tomb of King Tutankhamen ("Tut" to his friends). It was an extraordinary discovery made more remarkable because the tomb still contained most of its treasures. Filling the burial chamber were dismantled chariots, gilded figures, thrones—everything a king would need to support him in the afterlife. But Tut was a fool. He thought he could keep stuff that mattered to him. Wrong. King Tut left the building, yet his stuff remains. It's perpetually on tour now, like a 70s classic rock band.

The indignant brother who interrupted Jesus was also acting as a fool. Powerful lies shaped his world. Like an unholy blacksmith, these lies forged chains, bindings that linked his heart to his stuff and staked him to this world. The story Jesus told that day was meant to free him—and us—to see those chains; for those same lies can wrap around you and me.

Let's look at four covetous chains that bind our hearts to the world.

Chain 1: My Stuff Makes Me Happy

"You have ample goods laid up for many years," the parable's rich man told himself; "relax, eat, drink, be merry"

(Luke 12:19). In today's language his self-advice might be translated, "Shop, buy, and consume—and let it bring you happiness."

But does stuff really make anyone happy?

Certainly we all enjoy getting new things. But like the spoiled child on Christmas morning who surveys the carnage of a dozen newly opened toys and cries out for the one thing on his list he didn't get, stuff stokes desire and doesn't satisfy. Buy a TV, and coveting wants a DVD player. Buy a DVD player, and coveting wants cable. Buy cable, and coveting wants On Demand TV (a revealing concept in itself).

In Gregg Easterbrook's well-researched *The Progress Paradox: How Life Gets Better While People Feel Worse*, he notes:

> The incredible rise in living standards for the majority of Americans and Western Europeans has made them more affluent, healthier, more comfortable, more free, and sovereign over ever taller piles of stuff—but has not made them any happier.[5]

The happiness that comes from stuff functions much like a drug, creating a temporary sense of order or status that can become so intoxicating we need greater "stuff-hits" to maintain it. Our cravings to relax, eat, drink, and be merry can be a powerful temptation when we believe happiness is only a purchase away. Double-click on one popular retail web site, and the bestsellers include: A Quiet Power Motorized Tie Rack at $59 (to spare us those many hours we lose in searching for ties); a Musical Shower Companion at $199 (so we never have to bathe in silence again); and a Dyson Animal Vacuum at $499 (to, ah, hmm, vacuum animals I suppose).

To truly understand covetousness, we must understand that discontentment—the unhappy enemy within—forges its chains. Discontentment tells us that happiness will not occur until the next purchase, the next possession. It blithely dangles the carrot while we spend and spend to catch up. When we're discontented, cost or practical utility is rarely the point of a purchase. The point is the pursuit of happiness.

Early in our marriage, Kimm and I were living on the second floor of an old house. We didn't have a lot of extra space but found just enough on our small landing for a charcoal grill. Kimm loved grilling out and I loved eating what was grilled, so this marriage was destined to work.

Then some of our relatives and friends began purchasing state-of-the-art gas grills. Kimm and I found ourselves discussing our "need" for a gas grill we couldn't afford. There was nothing wrong with the grill we had; we'd just convinced ourselves a new grill would bring a deeper form of happiness. Fortunately, God got to our hearts before we got the new grill.

When we seek happiness in stuff, we find that no amount of it makes us happy. Life becomes earthbound and chained to things that are passing away. But when we resist the seducing whisper of worldliness, we discover eternal joy.

Chain 2: My Stuff Makes Me Important

For that man wanting part of his brother's inheritance, his approach to Jesus was not only crude but arrogantly self-important. If he took his mind off himself for a moment to listen to the parable Jesus tells, he would see himself in it. Perhaps he would consider the heady hubris of the rich man in that parable, each statement dripping with self-exaltation: "I will do this . . . I will do that . . . I will comfort my soul with my own wise words."

I . . . I . . . I . . . my . . . my . . . my . . . The rich fool lives in the world of All-About-Me.

Scripture has a specific name for this chain: pride in possessions. "For all that is in the world—the desires of the flesh and the desires of the eyes and *pride in possessions*—is not from the Father but is from the world" (1 John 2:16). *The New Bible Dictionary* comments on this passage:

> The two dominant characteristics of *"this* world" are *pride,* born of man's failure to accept his creaturely estate and his dependence on the Creator . . . and *covetousness,* which causes him to desire and possess all that is attractive to his physical senses.[6]

The intertwining of pride and covetousness is as inevitable as it is destructive. If I'm truly at the center of things (pride), then stuff exists to serve my desires (coveting). And if I find my identity in stuff (coveting), then the amount of stuff I acquire makes me important (pride). These dual chains are always strung together around anyone who finds self-importance in stuff.

How many advertisers seek to peddle their products by appealing to our inner arrogance, the unvarnished assumption being that we deserve the best? But pride is a ravenous rebel—it never ends there. Having obtained our desire, we then feel superior through that possession, wrongly assuming it says something wonderful about us. It's almost as if our purchase becomes a sacrifice we offer to ourselves: "Be exalted, you wonderful guy, through this offering of love!" Or, to say it more simply, my stuff makes me important.

Chain 3: My Stuff Makes Me Secure

In Jesus' parable, the economy was roaring and times were good: "The land . . . produced plentifully" (Luke 12:16). But the rich man's prosperity was merely the stage for the more important drama within his heart. Rather than a blessing, his abundance became a test—a test of where he was placing his trust.

He responded to the test with his own answer: "I will tear down my barns and build larger ones, and there I will store all my grain and my goods" (12:18). Good answer? Bad answer? It depends on what you trust.

Have you ever thought of prosperity as a test? Randy Alcorn once heard a leader of the persecuted church in Romania say, "In my experience, 95 percent of the believers who face the test of persecution pass it, while 95 percent who face the test of prosperity fail it."[7] Wow! That's a staggering statement. And I know one man who would agree.

David was born in Uganda, the eldest brother in a family of six. When David was thirteen, his father was killed and his family reduced to utter poverty. His mother provided for the family through itinerant labor and begging.

Through a series of miraculous provisions, David came to the United States to study and work. He has now lived here for more than a decade. Having walked the Christian life in the poverty of Uganda and in the prosperity of America, David has a unique perspective: "This may be confounding to you, but it was far easier being a Christian in the poverty of Uganda than in the affluence of the States. Prosperity tempts my laziness; it lulls me away from dependence upon the Lord. The affluence draws me toward passivity. It's a daily battle for dependence upon God versus dependence upon my own strength!" David learned quickly that prosperity is most dangerous because of its tendency to foster false security.

I can already hear the prayers almost daring God to make us the test-case: "Go ahead, Lord, test me with plenty—I can take it!" But not so fast. The rich man confronted the test of prosperity and finished with a failing grade. What hope do we have to do better?

Within us there is no hope. But because of the gospel we can stand confident in the outcome. Christ met and passed all the tests this world offers on his way to the cross. Where we fail, he was obedient. Where we stumble, he finished his race. The merit of that perfect obedience is transferred to us, and his death and resurrection have secured a place for us in God's favor, not in his judgment.

When we're tested—when we see that newer model of the old car we own, when we drive through that neighborhood of homes just a little nicer than ours, when we discover we can get a new computer twice as fast for half the money we paid two years ago—we have a place to go with our temptation to covet. We can go to the Savior who secured a place for us with God through the cross.

Chain 4: My Stuff Makes Me Rich

What a horrifying moment it would be to stand before God assuming you're rich only to discover your utter poverty. How could such a savvy businessman miss that little detail?

The rich man measured wealth incorrectly. He measured it by what was in his barns; God measured it by what was in his heart.

The rich man believed his stuff made him rich. That was why he hoarded, stashed, and stockpiled. Stockpiling is when we accumulate stuff and selfishly shelter it from others, so we never fear being without it. Like the rich man, we want to "build and store, build and store" without sufficient consideration for the purpose of our prosperity. We accumulate more than we need only to become blind and bloated by our blessing.

Can you relate?

Sadly, I sure can.

A number of years ago, a single mother in our church was returning to college. Since I had two book bags, my wife suggested that I give her one of mine. One was nice; the other was, well, not so nice. Which should I give her? What does good stewardship look like?

For me, at that time, it was a no-brainer. I gave her the used one. Why give her the good one? I might need it. After all, I did buy it. It was mine—my book bag . . . my *precious*!

When I look back, I see the ugly head of Gollum attached to my body. To my shame, I was offered an opportunity to share my prosperity, but instead I displayed the same chain as the rich fool. Pushing the Savior aside, I chose satisfaction in self. My decision was about protecting my stuff and keeping the best for me.

For the covetous heart, stuff always comes first. In a consumer culture, the obtaining and maintenance of stuff can determine our job choice, our leisure pursuits, our friendships, our house size, our local church. It can actually dictate the course of our lives.

Sadly, the rich man discovered that the stuff he owned now owned him. The very thing he most prized now became the cause of his demise.

When I was a kid, I watched the 1956 movie version of Herman Melville's *Moby Dick*. I remember little about the movie except the final scene. In it, Gregory Peck as Captain Ahab makes a last-ditch effort to harpoon his obsession, the great white whale. The harpoon strikes the whale, but unbeknown to Ahab the rope is wrapped around his leg. As the whale lunges in response to the piercing of the harpoon, Ahab is dragged overboard into the deep. The violent thrashings of the whale increasingly entangle the pitiable sailor and the beast. The last scene of Ahab remains indelibly marked in my memory—a helpless soul lashed by his own devices of his obsession, disappearing forever into the churning oblivion. The imagery is hauntingly clear. A man finally gets what he wants only for it to be the source of his destruction.

This picture gives us some sense of the utter futility of a life lived in covetousness and materialism. It describes the rich fool of the parable. It describes the man who interrupted Jesus. And maybe it describes you.

Covetousness chains the heart to things that are passing away.

If you're presently in the bondage of covetousness, there is good news: the chains of coveting, though strong, are not unbreakable. Because of the Holy Spirit within, we have the power to resist the seduction of this fallen world.

Christ engaged this man to show him the problem. It was an act of emancipation. Remember, the Son of Man came to deliver us from bondage to freedom.

Jesus followed this parable with a gracious discourse on the abundant provision of the Father, culminating in this extravagant promise: "Fear not, little flock, for it is your Father's good pleasure to give you the kingdom" (12:32). What a flabbergasting thing to say to all the covetous people around him. We of idol-tempted hearts, chained to things that are passing away, are promised an inheritance in a kingdom that will never pass away. How can this be?

It's because the One who exposes our coveting heart, the One who pronounces judgment on the unrepentant materialist, is himself the King of the kingdom. He has purchased the right by his own blood to give the kingdom to sinners who flee to him for mercy. And delighting in that is to start hungering for God more than for stuff. If covetousness chains the heart to what's passing away, the gospel is the key that frees the heart to seek what never passes away.

But there's something we need to do: remember the "Take care" exhortation from Jesus. How do we cherish gospel freedom while being on our guard against all covetousness?

Post Your Guard

Let us guard against covetousness by walking in grace, the abounding grace from God, that we might have "all sufficiency in all things at all times" (2 Cor. 9:8). We live in a materialistic world, but our hearts can be free from it. God wants to help us to post a guard over our hearts—a guard of gracious resolve.

Here are some ideas of what that guard should look like.

Consider Your True Riches

"For you know the grace of our Lord Jesus Christ, that though he was rich, yet for your sake he became poor, so that you by his poverty might become rich" (2 Cor. 8:9).

If you measure true wealth by material assets, you won't come out looking prosperous. Like everyone, you have more than some and not as much as many others. But if you measure your riches through what Christ did at Calvary—God's wrath appeased, our sin atoned, our soul redeemed—you're immediately transformed into the richest of the rich. Grace moved Christ to become poor so we could become wealthy. When the gospel gets big, covetousness becomes weak.

Are you feeling richer yet? Remember the words of John Owen:

> When someone sets his affections upon the cross and the love of Christ, he crucifies the world as a dead and undesirable thing. The baits of sin lose their attraction and disappear. Fill your affections with the cross of Christ and you will find no room for sin.[8]

Confess and Repent

Confess covetousness as sin, and set a course of repentance.

Covetousness can appear as a victimless sin. But it always

dishonors God. As author Thomas Brooks puts it, "All sin strikes at the holiness of God, the glory of God, the nature of God, the being of God, and the law of God."[9]

By allowing the true gravity and implications of our sin against God to soak in, we experience the conviction in our hearts that lays the groundwork for lasting change.

It's vital to note that the gospel is the motivator of our confession. The words of the apostle John are so helpful here: "If we confess our sins, he is faithful and just to forgive us our sins and to cleanse us from all unrighteousness" (1 John 1:9).

Because Jesus atoned for our sins on the cross, our confession finds favor with God our Father, and he pours out grace for change. Also, our confession need not be confined to God, particularly when we're members of a local church. James urges us, "Confess your sins [not just to God, but] to one another" (James 5:16). If we're enjoying biblical fellowship, that "one another" should begin with the circle of those affected by our covetousness, starting with family and extending to anyone in a legitimate position to serve us with their comfort and wise counsel. Embracing covetousness can be a private sin, but casting it off should be a group project.

Express Specific Gratitude

Understanding true wealth and confessing greed is a great start, but God wants to move us beyond an awareness of sin to live thankful for *all* he has done and *all* that we have.

This gratitude isn't something mystical that wells up inside of us after forty days of prayer and fasting. It's simply the obedient response of those who understand their heavenly assets. "Rejoice always . . . give thanks in all circumstances; for this is the will of God in Christ Jesus for you" (1 Thess. 5:16, 18).

Gratitude subverts greed. It's an expulsive antidote to covetousness in the heart. Gratitude is not a feeling, and it isn't based on present circumstances. It is recognition of our dependence on God and others—an act of humility that battles pride in our possessions. Grateful speech takes the attention off ourselves and places it on another, whether that's the God of our salvation or the spouse who washes our clothes. Gratefulness is recognition that God is always good and always right in his dealings with us. As the old hymn by Isaac Watts puts it:

> *O bless the Lord, my soul!*
> *Let all within me join,*
> *And aid my tongue to bless His Name*
> *Whose favors are divine.*
> *O bless the Lord, my soul,*
> *Nor let His mercies lie*
> *Forgotten in unthankfulness,*
> *And without praises die.*[10]

In times of plenty or need, the covetous heart says, "I want, I need, I will have." The grateful heart simply says, "O bless the Lord, my soul."

De-materialize Your Life

Recently a friend told me he and his family were "de-materializing" their house. I thought that was a great idea, right after I thought, "Hey, can I have your stuff?"

Kidding aside, it's painful. For them, it meant taking stock of their real needs by going through closets, attics, and storage to give away the stuff they don't need and don't use.

To the rich, Paul says, "They are to do good, to be rich in good works, to be generous and ready to share, thus storing up treasure for themselves" (1 Tim. 6:18–19). To those in our Western culture—those who own a home or drive a car and are exceedingly wealthy relative to the rest of the world—what changes do we need to make to better apply this passage and begin storing a different treasure? To de-materialize our lives will begin to hack away at the covetous chains in our hearts. But it won't be easy.

I know a guy who's an escape artist; I'm not making this up. His specialty is escaping from a straitjacket and a locked set of chains wrapped around his body. How does he do it? "No tricks. It's just work," is all he says. Seeing the discipline and effort required to systematically extract himself by contorting his body into slip knots, it looks like hard work. Afterward he's inevitably exhausted from the sheer effort it took to get free.

I think de-materializing our lives—the disciplined removal of the bondage of stuff—is something like this. No tricks, just work. Grace doesn't make things easy. But grace does make hard things possible.

Give Generously

Few things kill the coveting heart quicker than depriving it of stuff. Few things reflect the heart of God more than giving graciously.

Financial giving through tithes and offerings is a great start. It's designed to orient us toward stewardship by encouraging a lifestyle where resources flow through us. But this lesson moves beyond finances to our stuff. Peter talks about the orienting power of covetousness when he speaks of "those who have their hearts trained in greed" (2 Pet. 2:14). When it comes to materialism, we must unlearn what the world teaches. By his grace, God regularly reaches miserly people and transforms them into people of largesse.

One common fallacy that dazes some Christians is "virtual giving"—giving that occurs only in one's mind, if-things-were-only-different. "If I had more," we say, "I'd give more." That's virtual giving. In reality, if we had more we would undoubtedly find new ways to use it or store it.

When it comes to future blessing, God has a simple way to predict how deep we might dig: "One who is faithful in a very little is also faithful in much" (Luke 16:10).

When was the last time God was so big that you let go of a treasured possession to bless another person? I did it recently, and it hurt a little too much. More evidence that my stuff retains its grip, and I have a long way to go.

Parents: Guard and Guide Your Kids

The root of adult covetousness is planted in the child. It's best dug out before it takes hold. "I want" is said early and often in a child's life. Tantrums and sibling rivalry usually are little more than stuff wars. Unfortunately, parents often prefer the false peace of accommodation to the hard-fought victories of discipline. We've all seen it:

"Johnny got an orange one. I only got a yellow one! Why does he always get the orange one?"

"Johnny, can you let your sister have the orange one?"

"No, you gave it to me, it's mine!"

"Okay, honey, Johnny likes his orange one. How about this time you have the yellow one and next time you can have the orange one."

"I want the orange one now. It's not fair."

"Okay, here's a red one. Put them both in your mouth and they'll make an orange one."

"Why does she get two?"

How do we practically battle covetousness in our kids? Here are two strategies, one defensive and one offensive.

1) We need to defend our kids against the onslaught of advertising. Parents need to be on guard against "branding," a strategy for creating a strong allegiance in a consumer with a product or company. As Alissa Quart writes, "Teen-oriented brands now aim to register so strongly in kids' minds that the appeal will remain for life."[11]

Our children are exposed to thousands of ads per year, many of them targeted to incite covetous desires in their hearts. My wife and I have sought to teach our kids that advertising seeks to move desires within them and their wants from mere thoughts to needs and demands. As wants slide into the needs column, we gently remind them how advertising works hard to create an image or desire that's so strong it seems you have to buy the product immediately.

It's not about having the latest toy or clothes, though. It's a matter of the heart. We need to discern the effect of marketing on our children and defend them against its pervasive effect.

2) Offensively, let's teach our kids to share. Not in a negotiation: "Let him have it first, then you can have it." But instead, "Let him have it first and enjoy the act of giving." Beginning early with toys leads to a habit of sharing that, while not eradicating sin, will certainly provide opportunities to bring the gospel to bear on the clenched fist of covetousness throughout their childhood.

If you or your kids have a long way to go, don't be discouraged. Because of the cross, we learn that "he who began a good work in you will bring it to completion at the day of Jesus Christ" (Phil. 1:6). As we, by grace, delight in God and guard our hearts against covetousness, we'll see the chains loosen, and a freedom from the tyranny of stuff will grow in our lives.

So take heart! God has begun a good work. He will complete it.

Conclusion

We don't know what happened to the man in the crowd who interrupted Jesus that day. Did he carefully listen to the Savior? Or did he look for another judge? The Bible doesn't say.

But the following story is a true example of what *can* happen when a heart is set free from the chains of covetousness and materialism.

> January 5, 1976 was a day that neither I nor my wife will soon forget. It was the dead of winter in Dallas, Texas, and as the sun set, the temperature plummeted to well below

the freezing mark. I was in my third year of seminary stud-
ies and was up late reading.

"Fire!" The word rang out on that cold night with fright-
ening urgency, bringing me out of my chair and into the
parking lot of our apartment complex. There it was. Only
three doors away a fire was raging. My first reaction was
to awaken Ann and get her to safety. By the time she had
escaped and we had moved our car away from danger, the
fire department arrived and cordoned off the entire complex. In doing so they shattered any hope I had of rushing
back inside to save something of our possessions.

It was there in the parking lot at 11:00 PM, in sub-freez-
ing cold, that I learned an important lesson about myself.
The flames did more than simply light up the cold Texas
sky. They shone ablaze in my heart as well, dispelling the
darkness of sin's deceit. While mournfully contemplating
what would surely be the loss of all earthly possessions, it
suddenly struck me how attached I had become to material things. My sinful dependence on earthly goods was
exposed as I envisioned a future without clothes, without
furniture, and worst of all, without theology books. I was
shamed by the painful realization that my happiness was
so closely tied up with what I owned.

We frequently talk about Christ being all-sufficient,
but I fear that it has become little more than a theological
cliché. Though I had often affirmed this truth, I never
really knew that Jesus was enough, until He was all that I
had left. To be sure, I had my health; and my wife was safe.
But in one chilling moment in 1976 it suddenly clicked:
Jesus is not only necessary; He is enough.[12]

When covetousness seeks to chain the heart to things
passing away, grace empowers us to enjoy the One who is not

only necessary, but enough. And not just barely enough but overwhelming joy and satisfaction.

The Son of Man has come bringing the riches of the inheritance of God to all who receive him by faith. Unlike my sweatshirt, or any earthly entitlement, these riches of Christ are glorious (Eph. 1:8), immeasurable (2:7), unsearchable (3:8), imperishable (1 Pet. 1:4)—and ours forever!

Chapter Five

God, My Heart, and Clothes

C. J. Mahaney

WHEN IT COMES TO FASHION, I'm deliberately out of step. I don't care if what I'm wearing is trendy or not—in fact, it's my goal to resist the influence of others (from Paris or Hollywood or anywhere else) over my wardrobe. Like any man's man, I relish being *out* of style.

I want to feel comfortable in what I'm wearing, which is why my stained In-N-Out Burger T-shirt and old gray sweatpants are the most well-worn items in my closet second only to my single pair of jeans, which I wear any place a T-shirt and sweatpants would be inappropriate attire.

If you ever see me sharply dressed in public, it's only because my wife and daughters, out of great concern for my appearance, buy me clothes on my birthday and for Christmas.

My wife and daughters, in contrast to me, *do* care about what they wear. They are lovely women with impeccable taste. Each one has her unique style of dress, and I enjoy trying to find gifts that fit their individual styles.

"Adornment and dress is an area with which women are

often concerned," writes George Knight (who must have had teenage daughters). This is a good thing. God created women with an eye for making themselves and everything around them beautiful and attractive. But, as Mr. Knight goes on to observe, dress is also an area "in which there are dangers of immodesty or indiscretion."[1]

Many young women, though, are unaware of these worldly dangers. Several years ago I preached a message to our church from 1 Timothy 2:9 entitled "The Soul of Modesty." Eventually that message made its way into the hands of a young woman named Jenni. Prior to hearing my sermon, Jenni had no idea what God's Word said about the clothes she wore. "Modesty used to be a foreign word to me," Jenni later admitted in a testimony to our church congregation:

> My friends aptly nicknamed me "Scantily." When choosing what to wear I thought only of what would flatter me, what would bring more attention my way, and what most resembled the clothes I saw on models or other stylish women. I wanted to be accepted and admired for what I wore. I enjoyed my attire, the undue attention I received, and the way it stimulated my feelings.

Perhaps you can relate to Jenni. Maybe modesty sounds unappealing to you. If we played word association, you'd come up with "out of style" and "legalistic." Maybe you think God is indifferent about the clothes you wear. *What does he care?*

But as Jenni ultimately discovered, there is "not a square inch"[2] of our lives—including our closets—with which God is unconcerned. Even more, he cares about the *heart* behind what you wear, about whether your wardrobe reveals the presence of worldliness or godliness.

The evidence comes from 1 Timothy 2:9 where Paul urges "that women should adorn themselves in respectable apparel, *with modesty* and self-control, not with braided hair and gold or pearls or costly attire." Like 1 John 2:15 this is a verse we're inclined to ignore or reinterpret to escape its imperative. But we must not snip 1 Timothy 2:9 out of our Bibles. Rather, we must carefully seek to understand how it applies to our lives, our shopping habits, and the contents of our closets.

Now, this chapter is primarily written for women, not only because that's who 1 Timothy 2:9 addresses, but also because this is a topic of particular concern for women. George Knight is correct, and a woman's experience will tend to confirm the relevance and importance of this topic. However, modesty does have application for men—increasingly so in our culture. And especially for fathers, whose primary responsibility it is to raise modest daughters.

I write this chapter as the father of three daughters, now grown. I write as a pastor with a growing concern for the erosion of modesty among Christian women today. I write because God's glory is at stake in the way women dress. I write about modesty because God has first written about it in his eternal Word.

So let's take God to the Gap.

The Attitude of the Modest Woman

Any biblical discussion of modesty begins by addressing the heart, not the hemline. We must start with the attitude of the modest woman.

Worldliness

This emphasis on the heart is front and center in 1 Timothy 2:9. Note the phrase "with modesty and self-control." All respectable apparel is the result of a godly heart, where modesty and self-control originate. Your wardrobe is a public statement of your personal and private motivation. And if you profess godliness, you should be concerned with cultivating these twin virtues, modesty and self-control.

Modesty means propriety. It means avoiding clothes and adornment that are extravagant or sexually enticing. Modesty is humility expressed in dress. It's a desire to serve others, particularly men, by not promoting or provoking sensuality.

*Im*modesty, then, is much more than wearing a short skirt or low-cut top; it's the act of drawing undue attention to yourself. It's pride, on display by what you wear.

Self-control is, in a word, restraint. Restraint for the purpose of purity; restraint for the purpose of exalting God and not ourselves. Together, these attitudes of modesty and self-control should be the hallmark of the godly woman's dress.

In Paul and Timothy's day, modesty and self-control were foreign to many women walking through the local marketplace, just as they were to Jenni, and just as they are to the majority of woman at the local shopping mall today. And these concepts are certainly foreign to modern fashion designers, whose goal in clothing design is sensual provocation.

But for godly women, modesty and self-control are to be distinctly present in the heart. The question is, are they distinctly present in yours?

Such an attitude will make all the difference in a woman's dress, as pastor John MacArthur has observed:

How does a woman discern the sometimes fine line between proper dress and dressing to be the center of attention? The answer starts in the intent of the heart. A woman should examine her motives and goals for the way she dresses. Is her intent to show the grace and beauty of womanhood? . . . Is it to reveal a humble heart devoted to worshiping God? Or is it to call attention to herself, and flaunt her . . . beauty? Or worse, to attempt to allure men sexually? A woman who focuses on worshiping God will consider carefully how she is dressed, because her heart will dictate her wardrobe and appearance.[3]

Any conversation about modesty "starts in the intent of the heart." So consider for a moment: what is the intent of *your* heart in purchasing clothes to wear? Do a humble heart and a servant's heart dictate your wardrobe and appearance? Is your shopping informed and governed by modesty and restraint? Or is your dress motivated by a desire for attention and approval from others? Does your style reflect a lack of self-control?

There's an inseparable link between your heart and your clothes. Your clothes say something about your attitude. If they don't express a heart that is humble, that desires to please God, that longs to serve others, that's modest, that exercises self-control, then change must begin in the heart.

For modesty is humility expressed in dress.

The Appearance of the Modest Woman

What do humble, modest clothes look like? First Timothy 2:9 tells us: "Women should adorn themselves in respectable apparel . . . not with braided hair and gold or pearls or costly attire."

To better understand this verse, let's travel back in time to the early church. There had been some startling disruptions to the church's meetings of late, and Paul was writing to Timothy "so that . . . you may know how one ought to behave in the household of God, which is the church of the living God, a pillar and buttress of the truth" (1 Tim. 3:14–15).

Clearly, some people were *not* behaving in a manner worthy of the church of the living God, thus necessitating this gracious rebuke from the apostle.

Paul begins, appropriately, with the men: "I desire then that in every place the men should pray, lifting holy hands without anger or quarreling" (1 Tim. 2:8). He's saying, "Guys, quit arguing in church! You're distracting from worship, teaching, and prayer. Anger is always wrong but especially at church, the household *of God*, the church of the *living God*. So you need to stop fighting and start praying!"

Then Paul addresses the women in the verse we just read (1 Tim. 2:9). He is concerned because some of them are imitating the dress and adornment of the ladies of the Roman court and the prostitutes. Those women were known for their expensive clothes and jewelry and elaborate hairstyles; they dressed not only to attract attention but to seduce as well.[4]

When the women of the church arrived dressed like this, it's no surprise that they distracted others from worshiping God. What's more, through their ostentatious dress they associated themselves with the wealthy (thus separating themselves from the poor) and the ungodly (thus distancing themselves from their fellow church members). Their dress was distracting and maybe even divisive.

That's why Paul urges them to dress in "respectable apparel" and "not with braided hair and gold or pearls or costly attire." He wants the Savior, not seductive style, to be the focus of the church gathering—and indeed, the focus of all of life.

So the real issue wasn't actually braided hair, or gold, or pearls, or costly attire. The issue was—and is—clothing that associates with worldly and ungodly values: clothes that say "look at me" and "I'm with the world."

Let me be clear: Paul is not categorically prohibiting a woman from enhancing her appearance—on Sunday or any day of the week. In fact, you'll find other places in Scripture where godly women wore fine clothing and jewelry.

The woman of noble character in Proverbs 31 dressed in colorful and high-quality clothing (v. 22). Likewise the bride in the Song of Solomon adorned herself with jewelry (1:10). Esther had twelve months of beauty treatments (Est. 2:12). Obviously God isn't opposed to women making themselves beautiful.[5]

In fact, as my wife, Carolyn, has observed:

God is the creator of beauty. God delights in beauty. All we need to verify this fact is to consider the beauty He created all around us: whether it is an elegant flower, or towering trees, or a meandering river, or billowy clouds or the majestic night sky. Every time we stop to take in one of these breathtaking scenes on display in God's creation, we can't help but be convinced that He delights in beauty!

> Because we are created in the image of our Creator, each of us has this propensity to make things beautiful. That means, when we decorate our homes, or plant a lovely flower garden, or seek to add some form of beauty to our surroundings, even when we attempt to enhance our personal appearance—we are actually imitating and delighting in the works of our Great Creator.[6]

I admire my wife's feminine desire for beauty and her ability to make herself and her surroundings attractive. A woman can honor God by enhancing her personal appearance or by bringing beauty to her environment.

John Angell James agrees, with qualification:

> This taste [for beauty], however in many cases it may be altogether corrupted in its object, wrong in its principle, or excessive in its degree, is in its own nature an imitation of the workmanship of God, who, "by his spirit has garnished the heavens," and covered the earth with beauty.[7]

Mr. James is right. A woman's taste for beauty can be an imitation of God's character, but it can also become corrupted. And such was the case in this first-century church. Paul exhorted the women who professed godliness: "You should not dress in a way that resembles those who are extravagant, or worse, intent on being seductive or sexy. You must not identify with the sinful, worldly culture through your dress." Paul was writing not to condemn attractive attire but to address its corruption by association with worldly ideals and values.

This truth has timeless relevance. Consider who inspires

your attire. Who are you identifying with through your appearance? Who are you trying to imitate or be like in your dress? Does your hairstyle, clothing, or any aspect of your appearance reveal an excessive fascination with sinful cultural values? Are you preoccupied with looking like women at school or work or the actresses, socialites, and models on magazine covers, or the immodest woman next door? Are your role models the godly women of Scripture or the worldly women of our culture?

The women in the church should not look exactly like the ungodly, seductive women in the world. Women in the church are to be different. They should stand out not because of their revealing clothing but because of their distinctly modest heart and dress.

A Pastor's Concern

It's been almost two thousand years since Paul penned his letter, but 1 Timothy 2:9 remains a pastoral concern. Today, the issue is immodest and sensual clothing more than ostentatious attire. Immodest dress has greater potential for distraction in our church and in our culture. And it's no small challenge to address this matter. I know the great risk of offense or misunderstanding that I take by broaching this topic, the potential that you may feel I'm sinfully judging or wrongly accusing.

Please know that I don't write as a self-appointed critic. I am simply a concerned pastor who charitably assumes that most Christian women who dress immodestly are simply ignorant of the war with lust that men confront on a daily basis. They probably don't have a clue what goes on in a man's mind and what effect their bodies have on the eyes and hearts of men young and old.

But I want no one to be ignorant after reading this chapter. That's why I want you to hear from two young men who represent countless others. I hope their struggles and temptations—which are not unique but common to men— will motivate you to pursue modesty and self-control for the sake of your brothers in Christ. First, a day in the life of a college student pursuing purity:

Each and every day on campus is a battle—a battle against my sin, a battle against temptation, a battle against my depraved mind. Every morning I have to cry out for mercy, strength, and a renewed conviction to flee youthful lusts. The Spirit is faithful to bring me the renewal I need to prepare me to do war against my sin, yet the temptation still exists.

I'm thankful God has created me to be attracted to women; however, campus is a loaded minefield. There are girls everywhere, and I am guaranteed to pass some attractive girls as I walk to my classes. To make it through the day unscathed, I have to be actively engaging my mind— praying, quoting Scripture, listening to worship music, or looking at the sidewalk. Many days it takes all four to be safe.

The thing women do not seem to fully grasp is that the temptation toward lust does not stop; it is continual; it is aggressive; it does all it can to lead men down to death. They have a choice to help or deter its goal. Sometimes, when I see a girl provocatively dressed, I'll say to myself, "She probably doesn't know that 101 guys are going to devour her in their minds today. But then again, maybe she does." To be honest, I don't know the truth—the truth of why she chooses to dress the way she does. All I know is that the way she presents herself to the world is bait for my sinful mind to latch onto and I need to avoid it at all costs.

For the most part, the church serves as a sanctuary from the continual barrage of temptation toward sin. However, the church's members are not free from sin yet, and there are girls—those who are ignorant and those who are knowledgeable of men's sinful tendencies—who dress immodestly. I must confess that even church can have several mines scattered about.

To the girls who are ignorant: please serve your brothers in Christ and have your dad screen your wardrobe. Ask him how you can better choose holiness over worldliness. He's a guy, and he knows more about the temptations men face than you do.

And to the girls who don't follow the pattern of the world: thank you a million times over. You are following Scripture's commands and are helping your brothers in the process. Despite all that godly men are doing to defeat the sin of lust, they still need help, and they need you to provide it.

I commend this young man's tenacious fight for holiness. And I echo his gratitude to all women who choose to dress modestly—*thank you a million times over*. You're truly serving your brothers in Christ by your obedience to God's Word.

As Christian women in the church you can be either a blessing or a distraction, as the second young man explains:

Worldliness

The one place where I might think I wouldn't have to face as much temptation is at church, but this is not always the case. When women that I'm friends with dress immodestly, it definitely has a negative effect on our friendship. When a woman dresses immodestly, it doesn't make it easy to see her as a sister in Christ. There's a constant battle going on as I'm talking with her. Communication becomes more difficult because as I'm trying to listen to her, I'm also trying to fight temptation. I think some women aren't aware that even little things can distract guys a lot—showing even a little part of their stomach, wearing bags that have straps that go between their breasts, etc.

I'm so grateful for the friendships God has given me with the godly women in my church. I'm so appreciative of the sacrifices they make in order to glorify God and serve and care for the guys. I heard of one girl who went shopping and really liked the shirt she was trying on. But then she thought, "No, I can't do this to the guys." That was the first time I had ever heard of anything like that, and it made me so grateful. It is such a blessing to have friends who care for me enough to be selfless and to sacrifice what might look attractive in order to help me and other guys with sexual lust.

When women dress modestly, it's attractive and it makes me want to hang out with them more. I think modesty is so attractive and helpful in friendships because it makes it easier for a friendship to be centered around God and for fellowship to be unhindered.

Godly men find modesty attractive. They appreciate women who dress with self-control and restraint. They're grateful for women who serve them by helping them fight the temptation to lust.

After hearing about these young men's struggles, one young woman wrote to me:

> I had a vague idea that guys were more affected by sight than girls were, but I never realized how pervasive the temptation was. Now, knowing a little bit of what guys go through every day, I have an ardent desire to serve my brothers in Christ. I want to make the church a haven for them.
>
> Thanks to my parents' oversight, I don't think my wardrobe is immodest. But I can often spend too much time critiquing my outfit, trying to figure out how I can "work with what I have" to get guys' attention. After your message, I no longer have a desire to dress immodestly; rather, my concern is to protect the guys and help *them* in their walk with God. I don't want my clothes or behavior to distract them from focusing on God.

I hope this ardent desire to serve your brothers in Christ characterizes every woman in the church. But the church should also be a place where the unconverted can come dressed immodestly and be warmly welcomed, not self-righteously judged. Among Christian women, those who dress immodestly should be graciously corrected— not by self-righteous people trying to impose personal preferences, but by those who consider themselves to be the worst sinners they know and thus charitably assume ignorance on the part of the immodest. Modesty isn't the exclusive responsibility of the church's pastors and wives. It is the collective responsibility of all the members of the church.

A Word to Fathers

Dads, I want to urge you to take responsibility for your daughters' dress. Fathers are absolutely essential to the cultivation of modesty. When a young lady dresses immodestly, it usually means her father has failed to lead, care for, and protect her. Without a father's care and protection, she may be daily exposed to the lustful minds of men.

My three daughters are grown and married now, but from an early age I sought to impress upon them the importance of modesty. Before an article of clothing became a permanent part of their wardrobe, my girls had to get my approval. This wasn't always easy—for them or for me. Modest clothing is hard to find. Sometimes they'd arrive home after an all-day shopping trip only to hear me say, "That's not gonna work, my love. I'm so sorry, but exhaustion from shopping doesn't excuse immodesty. We're not going to compromise."

Here's what my daughter Nicole wrote about how my wife and I led her and her sisters:

> My parents were committed to raising modest daughters. They educated us about how men are stimulated visually. They examined any article of clothing that came into the house, giving it a thumbs up or sending us straight back to the store with the receipt. I'll admit it was frustrating to spend hours at the mall and have nothing to show for it. There were moments when that frivolous, selfish desire for cool, tight jeans overtook my desire to serve others. That's when Mom and Dad would remind me of the young men who were trying to glorify God. My clothes could either help or hinder them. When they put it like that, I was quickly saddened by my selfishness.[8]

We must not simply oversee our daughters' closets; we must teach them God's perspective of modest dress and educate them about the temptations of men. And we must have clear standards informed by Scripture, not by culture. This will make it easier for them to follow our leadership when difficult choices are necessary.

Author Nancy Leigh DeMoss provides two simple criteria for modesty: women should avoid "exposing intimate parts of the body" or "emphasizing private or alluring parts of the body."[9] My wife and daughters (at my request) have compiled more specific suggestions in their Modesty Heart Check (see Appendix A).

Ultimately, fathers, your job to raise a modest daughter culminates and concludes on her wedding day.

Several years ago my friend Lance Quinn asked me to teach at The Bible Church of Little Rock. One of the messages he asked me to share was on modesty. At the conclusion of the sermon, the church's worship pastor, Todd Murray, presented an additional appeal to the congregation. He urged all girls to consider modesty even when shopping for formal attire and wedding dresses. His words were laden with care and compassion, yet they carried an appropriate soberness. Here's a little of what he said:

> Ladies, please don't forget to apply these principles of modesty to formal events and weddings. In recent years I have become increasingly grieved by the immodest dresses of both brides and bridesmaids at the weddings that I officiate. I have observed a number of young ladies in our fellowship who have dressed modestly all their lives appearing on their wedding day in extremely provocative

dresses, exposing more of themselves than on any other day of their lives.

I assume the best about what is going on in the hearts of these young women. I don't think that they went to the wedding dress shop determined to be provocative. No doubt, they just wanted a dress that would be elegant on this day that they have dreamed of all their lives. When a bride and mother set out on their expedition to find a wedding dress, they are, quite naturally, thinking like . . . women! Unfortunately, there is no one in the shop who is thinking like a man.

I'd like to make a radical proposal, girls. Why not take your father with you to the wedding boutique? If that thought is just too much for you (or your dad!) at least consider taking the dress out on approval and allowing your dad to see it before you make your final purchase.[10]

Todd's proposal might be radical by cultural standards, but it is the biblical norm. The standard of modesty and self-control shouldn't change on your daughter's wedding day. If anything, it should be even more important to honor God on that momentous occasion.

Having three married daughters, I know the challenges involved in finding modest wedding attire. However, with a lot of time and effort, it can be done. As Todd mentioned, the dad's role is crucial in this process. I helped our daughters by providing guidelines for appropriate bridal wear as they went shopping with their mom and then giving final approval to their choices. (You can find helpful suggestions for a modest wedding ceremony in Appendix B.)

Once again, please be on guard against the temptation to be self-righteous toward those who choose differently. If you think a bride is dressed immodestly, her wedding day isn't the appropriate occasion to comment on her dress. Simply rejoice with her in the goodness of God displayed in her marriage.

But if you're a bride-to-be, or the father of a daughter who's preparing to get married, I hope these thoughts serve you in your effort to plan a ceremony that brings glory to God.

The Right Adornment

Notice in 1 Timothy 2 that Paul goes beyond addressing a woman's apparel. He desires "that women should adorn themselves . . . with what is proper for women who profess godliness—with good works" (2:9–10).

He's very clear about what makes a godly woman attractive. "Good works" are to be what's most noticeable about a woman who professes godliness. Not her wardrobe, but her good works—an observable lifestyle of serving others. That's the appropriate adornment for women who profess to be Christians. And it is one evidence of the transforming effect of the gospel.

This may mean less time applying makeup, styling hair, choosing clothes, and it may mean more time sacrificing on behalf of your family and your local church. Adorning yourself with good works means less time shopping and more time serving.

So, which are you more preoccupied with—shopping or good works?

Now, this is not a categorical criticism of shopping. The four women in my life think shopping is a gift from God. It's probably no surprise that I don't view shopping as favorably as they do. I would argue that shopping is actually a product of the fall. But that's because I'm a man. And as a man, I don't shop. If I go to the mall, it's to enter one store and buy one specific item. I'm not really "going to the mall"; I'm not walking in and out of various stores depending on what catches my eye. No. I'm on a mission to get a single item and then get out of there as quickly as I can.

For women, as I understand it, shopping can be a relaxing and enjoyable experience, a gift from God. But that gift, like any gift, can become an idol.

So which are you more passionate about—shopping or good works?

John Piper writes about coming across a review of the book *The Body Project* by Joan Jacobs Brumberg. This book looks extensively at a century's worth of changes in how girls view themselves. In the introduction, the author contrasts the diary of an adolescent in 1892 with that of a teenage girl in the 1990s. The girl in 1892 wrote this:

> Resolved, not to talk about myself or feelings. To think before speaking. To work seriously. To be self restrained in conversation and actions. Not to let my thoughts wander. To be dignified. Interest myself more in others.

The 1990s teenager wrote this:

> I will try to make myself better in any way I possibly can with the help of my budget and baby-sitting money. I will lose weight, get new lenses, already got new haircut, good makeup, new clothes and accessories.

The book's back cover summarizes what was true a century ago: "The ideal of the day . . . was inner beauty: a focus on good deeds and a pure heart." In contrast, the environment for girls today is "a new world of sexual freedom and consumerism—a world in which the body is their primary project."[11]

This cultural shift—from good works to good looks—parallels the departure from godliness to worldliness. Women who are professing Christians must be discerning enough to resist and reject that shift.

So, what are you consumed with—your clothing or your character? What are you known for—your good looks or your good works? If you're a mother, what is your daughter learning from you in this regard? She's surely studying you; as she does so, what is she learning—the latest fashions or good deeds?

Once again, let me remind you that the Bible doesn't forbid a woman from enhancing her appearance. But here in 1 Timothy 2:9–10, Paul isn't just advocating modesty in dress; he's insisting that more time and energy be devoted to spiritual adornment in the form of good works. And he's warning about excessive attention devoted to appearance to the neglect of good works.

The Modest Woman's Allegiance

Remember Jenni from the beginning of the chapter? A friend graciously confronted her immodest dress and encouraged her to take a closer look at what God's Word had to say about modesty. When Jenni pasted 1 Timothy 2:9 back into her Bible and began applying its truth to her heart and life, her perspective of modesty and her wardrobe underwent a complete transformation:

> When my friend expressed concern about my immodest dress and listed specific articles of clothing that drew attention to my body, I was sobered. *Lord, is it pride that motivates the way I dress? Does what I wear actually cause my brothers to stumble? Do I bring reproach to your name?* I immediately acknowledged my desperate need for God and began to plead for His mercy and grace to reveal the sin within my heart and assist me to change.
>
> I began to study God's Word, read material addressing this issue, and listen to C. J. Mahaney's teaching on "The Soul of Modesty." By the grace of God, there was no resistance in my heart but a passion to change. God illuminated the simple fact that it is my heart that dictates my appearance and wardrobe. I was faced with the question, "What statement do my clothes make concerning my heart?" The pride and ambition to exalt self were made very clear.
>
> I began to understand the heart and soul of modesty. Modesty is humility expressed in dress, a desire to serve others, neither promoting nor provoking sensuality or lust. It is rooted in a desire to lose any and all consideration of self and live hidden behind the cross of Christ. I became more and more aware that my dress was not an outward expression of the gospel or humility. I began by aggressively examining my wardrobe.
>
> My husband, Jon, and I spent a lengthy period of time examining every article of clothing, prayerfully considering which pieces were inappropriate. By the end of the examination my wardrobe had considerably diminished. To be honest, this has not been easy. Even though it has been a year since cleaning out my closet, there are still

many moments when I struggle picking out my outfit for the day, being dissatisfied with my limited wardrobe. It has been crucial for me to question my motives morning after morning, which helps me to see that what is most attractive is my desire to please God, not my outward appearance.

It is a daily fight to flee worldly desires and pursue godliness in this area. It requires daily application and frequent reminders. I have the "Modesty Heart Check" posted inside the bathroom vanity as a reminder every morning before I leave the house. I have identified specific areas where I am uniquely tempted and then spent time developing a plan to change. And when I purchase clothing, I always show my husband, Jon, to be sure that it is modest.

Dressing modestly blesses my husband because it is a way that I can save myself and my body for him alone. And it also serves the other men around me by helping to protect their hearts against temptation. By pursuing modesty in spirit as well as in dress, I can bring glory to Christ and further the gospel.

Some of you may wonder, like Jenni once did, why I make such a big deal about modesty, and more importantly, why Paul does. Is it because we're conservative people? Is it because we have personal preferences about how women should dress?

No. The reason is the gospel. Modesty is important because of the gospel of Jesus Christ. That's why Paul is concerned about it. He isn't simply a "cultural conservative." This isn't Paul's version of *The Book of Virtues*. For him, the issue of modesty is about the gospel.

And that's why you should be concerned about modesty

as well. For when we take a broader look at 1 Timothy 2:9, we discover that these instructions about women's dress are set in the context of the gospel:

> This is good, and it is pleasing in the sight of God our Savior, who desires all people to be saved and to come to the knowledge of the truth. For there is one God, and there is one mediator between God and men, the man Christ Jesus, who gave himself as a ransom for all, which is the testimony given at the proper time. (1 Tim. 2:3–6)

The gospel message is the motivation for modest dress.

The woman who loves the Savior avoids immodesty because she doesn't want to distract from or reflect poorly upon the gospel.

Bryan Chapell puts it like this: "Paul's overriding concern was that the way Christians deported themselves would not detract from but enhance their gospel mission."[12]

We have a gospel mission: not only to preach Christ but to live in a way consistent with our profession of faith. As women, you can actually detract from the gospel mission by dressing immodestly, or you can enhance the gospel mission by dressing in a way that reflects the transforming power of the gospel at work in you. The humble woman, the modest woman, is concerned about the lost. And her dress reflects that concern.

Make this your aim: that there be no contradiction between your gospel message and the clothes you wear. May your modest dress be a humble witness to the One who gave himself as a ransom for all.

How to Love the World

Jeff Purswell

I AM THE FATHER OF TWO BOYS, ages six and four. I'm forty-six. Right away you can spot my dilemma: so much wisdom to offer—so little energy.

My six-year-old, Samuel, presents a particular challenge in this regard. He's a human version of Tigger from the Winnie the Pooh tales: he's bouncy, trouncy, flouncy, pouncy, fun! Fun! Fun! Fun! Fun! (as I said, I'm a father of two young children). His top may well be "made out of rubber" and his "bottom made out of springs," for his waking hours are spent in perpetual motion. Sam's attachment to the ground is tenuous; he paces about on his toes, tossing his sinewy body around like a wrecking ball, often leaping from chair to sofa to countertop in an aerial obstacle course. Such physical turbulence reflects an equally active mind that generates endless ideas for games to play, inventions to build, and dramas to rehearse. Life is full. Life is fast. Life is fun.

But it's also exhausting.

On some evenings, my fatigue and selfishness combine to produce strings of terse, rapid-fire prohibitions: "Sam, stop

139

that. Sam, be careful. Sam, give that back to your brother. Sam, please don't stand on that. Sam . . . !" *Parenting by negation.* It grieves me now to picture the exasperated expression I've seen far too many times, an expression that seems to say, "But Dad, what *can* I do?"

You may be feeling something similar at this point in the book. Possessions. Television. Movies. Music. Clothes. Realities that surround us like the air we breathe, each category holding potential for compromise and soul-strangling sin. Much to be alert to. Much to be on guard against. Much to avoid. *The Christian life by negation.*

This book has sought to impart biblical discernment in areas that increasingly escape the scrutiny of an evangelical world so intent on "relating to the culture." For the Christian, the world is a battleground, filled with signs of humanity's rebellion against its Creator, which includes the remaining corruption in our own hearts. Discernment is, therefore, crucial. However, to read the message of this book as a call merely to avoidance is to misunderstand it. It would be tragic indeed if we ignored, diluted, or otherwise marginalized the command this book began with: "Do not love the world or the things in the world" (1 John 2:15). It would be equally tragic if we defined our relationship with the world simply in terms of negation. For John's Gospel affirms both God's love *for* the world (John 3:16) and his intention that we be *in* the world (John 17:18).

If previous chapters have encouraged us not to love the world, this final chapter will examine how we *should* love it, exploring ways Christians can live faithfully in this present age. What is our relationship to be with the world? How are we to relate to it? How can we imitate God's love for the world?

A comprehensive reckoning of the Christian life demands clarity on such questions, for it's in this world that the Christian life is lived.

The World: A Biography

Before we examine how we're to relate to the world, we must first understand it. We need a biblical worldview, a framework for understanding our human existence and environment that accords with reality.[1] Whether we're aware of it or not, each of us has a set of beliefs and assumptions about ourselves and about the world we inhabit. Through the lens of these beliefs and assumptions—our worldview—we interpret our experiences, draw conclusions, and make decisions. Ultimately, our worldview determines how we live. That's why it's critical that these beliefs align with Scripture, for only there do we find God's take on our lives, on this world, indeed on reality itself. The Bible sets forth the contours of our existence, answering fundamental questions about our identity, our environment, our relationships, our very purpose in life.

The Bible's depiction of reality comes to us by way of a story. It's the one, true, ultimate story that gives meaning to all our stories. It's the story of God and his saving activity toward his creation in general and humanity in particular.

A common summary of this story identifies four main moves in its plotline: *creation, fall, redemption, consummation*. Though we can't rehearse the whole story here, we can sketch a profile of these four "chapters" of it, extracting from them some essential themes that illuminate our existence in this world. If you're familiar with this story, I invite you to pull up a chair and listen to it again. It's a story we cannot hear too often or understand too well. For, more than a story, more than a history lesson, this narrative provides us with the only reliable interpretation of the cosmos, the meaning of history from the divine perspective, and a vision for life that guides our daily existence, imbuing it with significance and purpose.

Let the story begin.

Creation

This story's opening scene is foundational for all that follows. The first verse of Genesis casts its shadow over the rest of Scripture and the rest of history: "In the beginning, God created the heavens and the earth." This verse and the narrative that follows establish critical ideas that play out throughout the Bible's storyline.

What do we learn in this opening "chapter"?

God rules everything. Unlike the petty deities of ancient paganism, the transcendent God exercises his omnipotent will as the Bible's story opens, bringing into being all that exists. As a result, there are only two kinds of reality in the world: God and everything else. Only God is eternal; everything else came about by his purposeful creative activity. And what God made, he has the prerogative to rule. Far from being autonomous from God, we and all of creation owe allegiance to him. Therefore, the scope of his reign is as vast as the cosmos.

God created us to fellowship with him in this world. As

God's creative fiats majestically unfold, adorning the entire cosmos, the narrative slows as it reaches creation's pinnacle: the creation of mankind. Man's creation is described in terms stunningly different from the rest of the universe: "Then God said, 'Let us make man in our image, after our likeness. . . .' So God created man in his own image, in the image of God he created him; male and female he created them" (Gen. 1:26–27). This language sets apart mankind—both men and women—from the rest of the material universe. Humanity was created to live in fellowship with God, representing him within the creation and reflecting him to creation.

The created order is good. Woven throughout the creation narrative in Genesis 1 is this sixfold refrain: "God saw that it was good." The chapter concludes with God's final, emphatic assessment: "And God saw everything that he had made, and behold, it was very good" (1:31). Contrary to any notion that denigrates the physical world or that carves up reality into sacred versus secular, spiritual versus non-spiritual, the Bible affirms the entire creation as a good gift from God, existing for his glory.

Fall

The entrance of sin into the world shattered the idyllic setting of Eden, and the consequences continue to be devastating. Here we learn what has gone wrong with the world in which we live.

Sin disrupts man's relationship with God. Adam and Eve, created to know and love God and respond to him in trusting dependence, instead rebelled and asserted their autonomy. Consequently, they were cast out of Eden, the garden-temple where they experienced fellowship with their Creator. Such is the story of mankind ever since. Fallen men and women—you and I—reject God's authority and seek to rule ourselves. Created to worship God, we instead become idolaters and set our hearts on things in this world.

Sin disrupts human relationships. In the wake of the fall, human relationships disintegrated. Self-centered shame splintered the one-flesh union of marriage, and vindictive violence demolished the first sibling relationship. Thereafter, "man's inhumanity to man" has characterized the story of human history.

Sin infects the entire creation. Even the non-human creation suffers the consequences of Adam's sin. Created to be the sphere of man's rule, the material world now resists man and becomes a source of hardship for him (Gen. 3:17–19), "groaning" under the effects of the fall (Rom. 8:20–22). Sickness, crime, poverty, injustice, suffering, death—this is not the way the world is supposed to be. And mankind's sin is the culprit.

Redemption

The rest of the Bible portrays God's activity to redeem mankind and creation from the guilt and ravages of sin. God did not relinquish his good creation to Satan and evil but decisively acted to set all things right again, to the praise of his glorious grace.

God promises to conquer sin and remove it from his creation. The first hint of salvation comes in the immediate wake of Adam's sin, as God intervened to create a hostility between evil and mankind (Gen. 3:15). History is therefore marked by conflict between "the seed of the serpent" and "the seed of the woman"—those who rebel against God and those who respond to him in faith and obedience. A day is coming, however, when the ultimate seed of the woman will finally triumph over sin and quell all rebellion in the world.

God works in history to reveal himself to sinners and gain a people for himself. From Genesis 3 onward, the Bible portrays God progressively working to accomplish his redemptive purposes. As this drama unfolds, the contours of his saving intentions gradually crystalize. The promises to Abraham in Genesis speak of the universal blessing that will come through Abraham's descendents. The liberation of the Hebrews from Egyptian bondage typifies God's intention to deliver his people from the bondage of sin. The forging of the nation of Israel reveals God's desire to have a people for his own possession. Israel's sacrificial system reinforces God's uncompromising holiness and points to an ultimate sacrifice that will atone for sin. The Davidic monarchy expresses God's loving rule over his people and establishes a pattern for an ultimate King who will shepherd the people of God in faithfulness. The prophets anticipate a time when God will act decisively to bring the fullness of his reign, a reign that will bring final judgment upon all evil and a final salvation encompassing all the earth. Although sin continues to mar humanity, God's saving purposes relentlessly barrel forward.

The climax of God's saving activity arrives in the person of Jesus Christ. All the promises given and the hopes expressed in the Old Testament find their fulfillment in Jesus. In his person, the much-anticipated reign of God has come to the earth. In his incarnation, God himself came to dwell among and reveal himself to his people. His blameless life achieved the perfect righteousness a holy God requires. His sacrifice on the cross absorbed God's righteous wrath and provided payment for sins—mankind's cosmic treason. His resurrection heralded the arrival of the first installment of God's redemption of his entire creation. Christ conquered sin, death, Satan, rebellion, and corruption. The restoration of all things has begun!

Consummation

The conclusion of the Bible unveils the goal of history and the final realization of God's purposes. The redemption of man and creation accomplished by Christ on the cross will be finally and fully revealed.

God's people are gathered. The gathering of the elect before the throne of God from every corner of the globe (Rev. 7:9–10) fulfills God's purpose to gather for himself a people for his own possession. Man is forgiven and restored to his Creator.

God's creation is renewed. The "new heaven and new earth" of Revelation 21 depict the restoration of all things. God will eradicate sin and all its destructive effects from the entire creation. Creation itself will be restored to its original goodness.

God dwells among his people. In the New Jerusalem, there will be no temple, "for its temple is the Lord God the Almighty and the Lamb" (Rev. 21:22). In the descent of the New Jerusalem, there's a joining together of heaven and earth, so that man —forgiven, restored, and glorified—can dwell face-to-face with his Creator. The goal of salvation-history is realized: God dwells with his redeemed people in a renewed creation.

What a story! The grandness of its scale, the integrity of its parts, the clarity of its moral vision, the nobility of its themes, and the authenticity of its narrative dwarf the greatest accomplishments of literature. What's more, it's all true! It conforms to reality. It elucidates the human predicament. It explains the world. It makes sense of our lives. There's no dimension of reality it doesn't embrace, no sphere of human existence it doesn't touch, no aspect of our lives it doesn't address. Here we find clarity for our lives, direction for our activities, and hope for our future.

Equipped with these fundamentals of a biblical worldview, let's turn now to consider our relationship with the world. Drawing from the Bible's storyline, I'd like to suggest three God-given tasks that give substance to our interaction with the world in which we live.

Task 1: Enjoy the World

This might seem a surprising category in a book about worldliness, but as C. J. made clear in chapter 1, worldliness is not a matter of *matter*, but of the *heart*. The "world" we're forbidden to love (1 John 2:15) is not the earthly creation but the rebellious, independent, God-rejecting mindset of those who inhabit this creation. It is mankind in settled opposition to God. Therefore, we must not share this world's outlook, live by its values, cherish its cravings, or pursue its goals. There's an old hymn that proclaims, "This world is not my home." Ethically speaking, this is true. We're "strangers and exiles" (Heb. 11:13) in a fallen world intent on self-exaltation and dedicated to self-indulgence. In this sense, we must not "love the world," setting our hearts on that which is opposed to God.

Geographically speaking, however, this world, in an ultimate sense, *is* our home. God created it for us, he delegated its development and care to us, and at the consummation he will dwell here with us forever following our resurrection and the world's renewal after Christ's return (Rev. 21:14). Through the lens of a biblical worldview, the material world takes on entirely new dimensions, with new purposes and possibilities for our lives. One of those possibilities is an enhanced enjoyment of the world. As a fellow-heir with Christ of the world, a Christian's enjoyment of it should be deeper, more authentic, more satisfying, and more enduring than that of those who have no share in this inheritance.

This enjoyment is rooted in two solid realities.

Creation Is God's Witness

"The heavens declare the glory of God, and the sky above proclaims his handiwork" (Ps. 19:1). According to David, the created world isn't simply there; it speaks. Everywhere we look, the world around us bears witness to the Creator, who brought it into existence. As T. M. Moore puts it, "Created things are ambassadors of glory from God to His people."[2]

David goes on in Psalm 19 to describe the massive scope and magnitude of the creation's communication:

> Day to day pours out speech, and night to night reveals knowledge. There is no speech, nor are there words, whose

voice is not heard. Their voice goes out through all the earth, and their words to the end of the world. (19:2–4)

A veritable deluge of revelation floods the world from end to end. Commenting on the universality of creation's witness, John Calvin observes that God "revealed himself and daily discloses himself in the whole workmanship of the universe. As a consequence men cannot open their eyes without being compelled to see him."[3] When you open your eyes, what do you see? According to Scripture, we should be seeing God. And we should see him *everywhere*—in the "whole workmanship of the universe." Creation's witness is profuse and inescapable.

Moreover, creation doesn't simply give us the vague impression that God is somehow out there somewhere ("He *must* be there; look at all this stuff!"). True, creation testifies to his reality, but it does more: it communicates real things *about* God. In speaking of God's general revelation in nature,[4] the apostle Paul notes:

> For what can be known about God is plain to them, because God has shown it to them. For his invisible attributes, namely, his eternal power and his divine nature, have been clearly perceived, ever since the creation of the world, in the things that have been made. (Rom. 1:19–20)

According to Paul, we can discern certain things about God through what he has made. Roaring seas proclaim his might, towering peaks bespeak his majesty, variegated wildflowers whisper of his complexity. In these and a million other ways, "the things that have been made" testify to the nature of the One who made them.

Of course, not everyone acknowledges creation's testimony about God. In the text just quoted, Paul diagnoses this failure. Fallen people "suppress" the truth of God that has been revealed to them (Rom. 1:18), and in their ingratitude they turn from God to find meaning, security, and satisfaction in the creation rather than the Creator—the essence of idolatry (Rom. 1:21–25). But the miracle of the new birth, which grants eyes of faith to see the "light of the knowledge of the glory of God in the face of Jesus Christ" (2 Cor. 4:6), also opens blind eyes to perceive the handwriting of God in creation, which points beyond itself to its Source and Sustainer.

Creation Is God's Gift

The second reality that anchors and informs our enjoyment of creation is the sheer fact that God gave creation to us to enjoy. In the creation narrative, God locates man in a place of rich provision and enjoyment designed specifically for him. The name Eden itself means "pleasure" or "delight," and Scripture uses the language of plenty, richness, and pleasure to describe its landscape. In the garden was "every tree that is pleasant to the sight and good for food" (Gen. 2:9).[5] From the beginning, God intended man to experience fellowship with his Creator in a beautiful, unblemished environment.

Although the fall brought frustration and corruption even to the natural creation, it remains a gift from God to be acknowledged, appreciated, and enjoyed. Indeed, as the Bible's story demonstrates, God is committed to the material world and his redeeming work embraces it. In his rebuke to those who would denigrate the natural world and its pleasures, the apostle Paul affirms, "For everything created by God is good, and nothing is to be rejected if it is received with thanksgiving, for it is made holy by the word of God and prayer" (1 Tim. 4:4–5).

When Paul warns the wealthy about the deadly temptations of riches, in the same breath he also affirms the joy-giving potential of the physical world: "As for the rich in this present age, charge them not to be haughty, nor to set their hopes on the uncertainty of riches, but on God, who *richly provides us with everything to enjoy*" (1 Tim. 6:17). It may sound strange to ears tuned to discern danger in all talk about "the world," but Paul seems just as concerned about a failure to appreciate creation as he is about the tendency to worship it. To be sure, sin has worked its mischief in the natural world; the physical creation itself was "subjected to futility" (Rom. 8:20), and sinful humanity persists in its relentless worship of the creation to the exclusion of the Creator. So we must guard the affections of our hearts with vigilance. But for the heart transformed by the gospel, the physical world holds great promise as a worship-producing source of pleasure and provision that opens the eyes to God and engenders worship of God.

If creation is both God's witness and gift, we have the dual responsibility of studying and enjoying the world around us. Such activities are part of what it means to glorify God as his image bearers. Fulfilling this call will have at least three specific, God-glorifying effects in our lives.

Knowing God. Since the creation reveals God, we can expect diligent observation of the world to yield a deeper knowledge of God. Of course, knowledge of God gained exclusively from observation of the natural world will always be partial at best, and it can never impart a saving knowledge of God. We need the particular revelation of Scripture to disclose the saving purposes of God in the gospel, as well as to confirm, clarify, and correct our perceptions of the natural world. But armed with the teaching of the Bible and working in concert with it, our experience of the physical creation can broaden and strengthen both our grasp of our Creator as well as our enjoyment of him.

Let me suggest some examples.

I love chocolate—rich, dark chocolate that snaps cleanly in your fingers, sits velvet-like on the tongue, and mingles bitterness with sweetness as it progressively reveals its flavors throughout your mouth. Now, my description of the joys of chocolate might be illuminating (or concerning) to you, but experiencing the chocolate yourself would be an entirely different experience.

In a faintly similar way, experiencing God's revelation in nature deepens and expands our understanding of the truth of Scripture.[6] The vibrant, multihued splendor of clouds framing a sunset palpably nourishes my soul and enriches my grasp of God's beauty. The intricate complexity of a cell under a microscope dazzles my imagination and deepens my appreciation for God's wisdom. The ear-numbing roar of a crashing waterfall confronts me viscerally with God's power. The serenity of bulging, motionless clouds on a still summer day halts the traffic of my mind with God's peace.

In each case, my experience of the natural world powerfully impresses upon me an aspect of scriptural truth. Each second of every day creation proclaims, and through its proclamation enhances our understanding and experience of the God who made and sustains it and who reveals himself to me through it.

Imitating God. In Ephesians 5:1 we read, "Therefore be imitators of God, as beloved children." Although we fulfill this command most directly as we demonstrate sacrificial love toward others (5:2), moral categories don't exhaust this verse's application. The physical world offers abundant opportunities for God's image bearers to imitate him, and by so doing to glorify him by reflecting his nature and character. When an artist brings beauty out of oil paint or clay, she bears witness to the Craftsman who imagined the universe. The golfer who launches a drive 350 yards down the center of the fairway reflects the prowess of Providence. The singer whose aria makes the hair on your neck stand on end conveys hints of transcendent Beauty.

Of all people, it is the Christian who should appreciate aesthetics, discerning with renewed powers of perception the handiwork of God in creation. And as our own aesthetic achievements reflect his creativity and skill, we join him in expressing and celebrating beauty—a beauty that points us to God and intensifies our delight in him.

Delighting in God. The more we learn of God's world and his works, the more cause we have to delight in God and express his praise. The psalmist's experience confirms this observation:

> O Lord, how manifold are your works! In wisdom have you made them all; the earth is full of your creatures. Here is

the sea, great and wide, which teems with creatures innumerable, living things both small and great. . . . I will sing to the LORD as long as I live; I will sing praise to my God while I have being. (Ps. 104:24–25, 33)

All sorts of endeavors hold great potential in this regard, from the scientist who solves a mystery of microbiology to the child who marvels at a firefly. The discovery of new places, the enjoyment of the world's vast variety, new sights, new sounds, new smells, new tastes—God's creation is filled with experiences awaiting to delight our hearts and to elicit praise to the God who made them.

Task 2: Engage the World

This second God-given task relates to our call to involvement with the world. After Scripture records the creation of man and woman in the image of God in Genesis 1, God immediately issues to them his first command:

And God blessed them. And God said to them, "Be fruitful and multiply and fill the earth and subdue it and have dominion over the fish of the sea and over the birds of the heavens and over every living thing that moves on the earth." (Gen. 1:28)

As those uniquely created in the image of God, mankind has received the astonishing privilege of filling and governing the natural world on God's behalf.

In Eden, we see some of the dimensions of God's original command spelled out: "The LORD God took the man and put him in the garden of Eden to work it and keep it" (Gen. 2:15).

Humanity's responsibility is twofold. First, we're to "work" the earth, tilling its soil, developing its potential, marshalling its resources for mankind's good. Second, we're to "keep" it, responsibly stewarding the earth, protecting it from evil and abuse. Although all that God made was "very good" (Gen. 1:31), it wasn't complete; God delegated the development of his good creation to his image bearers. This development includes not simply the earth itself, but also the vast array of cultural possibilities that God built into the natural order, including family, science, commerce, technology, government, and the arts.

Theologians refer to this original command as the "creation mandate" or "cultural mandate," and this noble calling remains in force today. Although sin's entrance into the world has rendered this task far more difficult, it did not revoke the mandate (see Gen. 9:1). Caring for and developing the world isn't simply a necessary chore, a sub-spiritual add-on to our otherwise meaningful lives—far from it. "Subduing the earth" is intrinsic to our very humanity as God's image bearers and an essential way that we serve and glorify God.

Recognizing this should demolish any distinction in our thinking between sacred and secular spheres of our lives. We're all plagued by the tendency to compartmentalize some aspects of our lives as spiritual, good, and holy and others as unspiritual, unimportant, and amoral. Perhaps you're familiar with this impulse: "God really cares about my devotions, my church involvement, my tithe, and my sharing the gospel. Those are important. But my work? Just a necessary evil. Home responsibilities? They've got to get done. My free time? That's *my* time (as long as I don't sin)."

Such thinking demeans Christ's lordship and impoverishes our spiritual life, rendering our faith irrelevant to 98 percent of our daily existence. No wonder so many lack passion in their Christian lives.

A biblical worldview sees every moment of life lived under the sovereign grace of God and the enabling power of the Holy Spirit. Scripture's story is emphatic: God's rule extends to all of creation and therefore to all of our lives. As Abraham Kuyper famously put it, "There is not a square inch in the whole domain of our human existence over which Christ, who is Sovereign over *all*, does not cry: Mine!"[7]

Therefore, every second of life is significant. All the diverse activities implied by the cultural mandate are good and worthwhile and pleasing to God. A biblical worldview gives us new eyes to see *all* of life: every sphere is charged with potential, every activity providing an opportunity to serve God, encounter God, obey God, enjoy God, testify to God, and bring glory to God. Because God is sovereign over all things, and Christ is redeeming all things, *all things matter to God*.

Let's briefly consider how this perspective should impact our involvement with the world.

Work

The rat race. The daily grind. I'm off to the salt mines. Thank God it's Friday. Clichés like these capture our culture's bleak view of work. We endure labor as a necessary evil that yields the reward of leisure. Perhaps we worship work as an avenue of self-exaltation or an escape from the tedium of an otherwise empty life. Some Christians are more "spiritual" about it: for them, the workplace provides opportunities to witness and money to pay tithes. But beyond that we're pretty much just biding our time. After all, secular work is a second-class calling that enables ordinary Christians to support those doing the *really* important work of full-time Christian ministry.

The biblical worldview delivers us from the dreary existence that such thinking produces. Far from being a necessary evil, work—which preceded the fall (Gen. 2:15)—is part of God's good creation, a noble calling that reflects the dignity of bearing the image of the Creator. As a result, our jobs aren't something to be endured until we can *really* serve God (at church, on a missions trip, or until we can get a job at a Christian organization)—they *are* serving God! They're a channel by which we help to fulfill the cultural mandate, contributing our gifts and labors to those of others to develop and protect God's creation.

The significance of our work is multifaceted. For example, *work is a primary way we imitate God.* God is a worker. In fact, Scripture patterns our work as well as our rest on the rhythm of God's own work and rest in creation (Ex. 20:8–11). When we cultivate and demonstrate skill through a complex computer program, an innovative architectural design, or a business plan that comes in under budget, we're reflecting the skill of God who does all things well.[8]

In addition, *work is a primary way we serve others.* Do you labor with this awareness? A builder's house provides shelter. A farmer's produce provides sustenance. An assembly worker's car provides transportation. A journalist's article provides awareness of important developments in a community. A sanitation worker provides a clean environment. Manufacturing, accounting, engineering, transportation, entertainment—all the facets of a society's network of relationships work together, under the common grace of God, to supply society's needs. Diligent labor is a tangible way we obey our Lord's command: "You shall love your neighbor as yourself" (Matt. 22:39).

Related to this is the fact that *work is a primary way we're used by God*. You might nod in agreement: "Yes, I should glorify God in my work." But do you realize God is using you in your work? Indeed, he is present in your work.

Martin Luther observed that a person's vocation is a "mask of God"—God cares for his creation and provides for his creatures' needs through the hands and labors and efforts of people.[9] So the farmer doesn't just sow and reap; God provides food through him. The lawyer doesn't just try a case; God executes justice through him. The trucker doesn't just drive a route—God distributes products through him. However oblivious people may be to this reality, God's kindness pulses through their daily activities, investing them with nobility and working through them to shower innumerable blessings upon undeserving sinners like you and me.

So don't just "go to work" and "do your job"—see your job as a way to imitate God, serve God, and love others. This doesn't mean work will never be difficult or frustrating or tedious; the curse ensures that it will be at times. But God's creational purposes and Christ's redeeming work infuse our work with meaning, and promise God-glorifying fruit as a result.

Home

The biblical idea of vocation or calling doesn't end with our jobs. A Christian has many callings in various dimensions of life, and none is more important than the home. In a family, fatherhood isn't a mere biological function or a task; it's a calling from God. The same is true for motherhood. Likewise, being a son or daughter is a calling from God. Why is this important? Because even the most ordinary, mundane details of our home life are sacred callings from God, to be pursued with faith and dependence upon God's enabling power. From family meals to household chores, from home improvements to game nights—no dimension of home life is exempt from Christ's loving lordship.

As a husband who daily observes the unflagging labor and selfless sacrifice of my wife, Julie, as she cares for me, our two boys, and our home, I carry a particular burden that mothers grasp and, amid the unremitting responsibilities and countless chores of parenting, remember this message. Despite our culture's pervasive hostility to the idea, motherhood is a calling from God, and no calling is higher. Although Scripture calls husbands to provide loving leadership to their homes, it's the incessant labors of mothers that, day by day, year after year, instill biblical values and inculcate a Christian culture in the home. Who can measure the long-term effects of nurturing helpless infants, supervising wandering toddlers, disciplining self-willed children, and counseling self-absorbed adolescents? Of family outings planned, traditions built, memories made, books read, songs sung, Scripture taught? That's why motherhood belongs under the heading, "Engage the World"; no one shapes generations or fashions cultures more than mothers.

Worldliness

All of Life

The above paragraphs are merely suggestive examples of how the storyline of Scripture calls us to engage the world in every area of life. Other areas could be considered.

Think about the years spent in education. Far from being a holding pattern until we get into the "real world," education is a means to glorify God. Of course, it can—and, in perhaps most cases, it will—prepare me for vocation, but more fundamentally it's a way to love God with all my mind. It alerts me to observe the works of God in creation and history. It equips me to enter into the conversation going on in culture, bringing to that conversation biblical discernment and wisdom. It prepares me to serve others by developing my mind and my gifts and my interests, using all these in the responsibilities God assigns to me and the opportunities he affords me.

What about leisure? For many in our culture, leisure and entertainment are mere distractions, often idolatrous ones. But for the Christian, leisure is a *sign*—a foretaste of the fullness of joy and richness and rest that awaits us in the new heavens and new earth. We're not robots designed for maximum operating efficiency in strictly utilitarian endeavors. God made us to know him and glorify him forever. Leisure reminds us of this and offers us a taste of this eternal calling in the here and now of this world.

What about the third of our lives spent in sleep? This, too, is a gift from God designed to inform and temper our active involvement in the world. Sleep is not mere inactivity, a brief respite from the important work we have to do in life. Sleep reminds us that God is God and we are not; only he "will neither slumber nor sleep" (Ps. 121:4). As we lay down our weary heads, we're forced to relinquish the illusion of control over our lives and to entrust ourselves to the Lord, who keeps us in all our ways. Ultimately, sleep and rest point us to the rest that finds its fulfillment in the gospel of Jesus Christ, the great rest-giver (Matt. 11:28–30) whose sacrifice on the cross frees us from the futile efforts to atone for our sin, to overcome our depravity, and to commend ourselves to God.

The story of the Bible insists that God's reign extends to every part of creation—indeed, to every facet of our lives. Do you live with such an awareness? This is the point of the apostle Paul's startling metaphor for the Christian life: "a living sacrifice" (Rom. 12:1). Every breath offered to God. Every moment lived for God. Sobering? Yes. But also breathtaking. Think about it. All of life affords one long opportunity to experience God, to serve God, to be used by God, as we receive from him our gifts, callings, and opportunities and the power to utilize them for his glory.

Task 3: Evangelize the World

This final point may strike you as a bit predictable (like the first two tasks, it even begins with an *E*). It's also likely to elicit the inevitable guilt most of us experience when the subject is broached. Raise the topic of evangelism, and most sincere Christians will nod their heads, even as their eyes look down and their feet shuffle in embarrassment. It need not be this way, however. Once again, a biblical worldview can transform evangelism from a neglected Christian duty or a mark of elite spirituality to an exhilarating privilege for every believer.[10]

Recall the Bible's storyline we began with: *creation, fall, redemption, consummation.* As Christians, it's critical that we locate ourselves within this story, for this will inform and guide the nature of our involvement with the world. We live in that period of salvation history between the redeeming work of Christ on the cross—where sin was atoned for and Satan's stranglehold on humanity was broken—and the consummation of God's saving plan, when Christ will return to earth, Satan and all his works will be vanquished, and God will dwell with his people in a transformed creation. Until that glorious day, Christians have the consummate privilege of being God's ambassadors in a fallen world, proclaiming to sinful men and women the stupendous news about Jesus Christ and the way of salvation through him.

This cosmic vantage point should bring fresh perspective and motivation to a task we often shy away from. Far from being an optional extra of the Christian life, evangelism lies at the core of God's campaign to restore his entire creation—the reconciliation of his rebellious image bearers to himself. The unfolding of salvation history has therefore expanded the job description of God's people. In addition to filling and subduing the earth (Gen. 1:28), God now calls us to "Go . . . and make disciples of all nations" (Matt. 28:19) through the proclamation and teaching of the gospel. These two facets of the Christian life are in fact inextricably related: the redemptive mandate of the Great Commission makes the fulfillment of the creation mandate possible. Only through Christ's redeeming work can God's redemptive purposes for this world be realized.[11] To be sure, through common grace God restrains much evil and bestows many blessings to humanity. However, apart from the power of the gospel to transform human hearts and redirect human lives to live for God's glory, man would never comprehend or realize the purpose for which he was created: "to glorify God and enjoy Him forever."[12]

Each of Us and All of Us

The privilege of evangelism has both an individual and a corporate dimension. The last recorded words of Christ endow every Christian with a noble identity and high calling: "You will be my *witnesses*" (Acts 1:8). Of course, Jesus' apostles were uniquely witnesses of his life and resurrection, and their proclamation launched the church's mission to spread the gospel to the ends of the earth. But this term wasn't limited to the apostles, nor were they the only ones who proclaimed the gospel in the book of Acts. Stephen before the Sanhedrin (Acts 6–7), Philip in Samaria (Acts 8), nameless Christians in Antioch (Acts 11:20), countless believers throughout the centuries, you and I—we all bear the privilege and responsibility of communicating the message of the gospel to those around us.

The word *witness* doesn't originate in religious contexts or in evangelism materials. As in its common legal usage today, the word simply speaks of one who provides testimony of something they've seen or experienced. In a law court, a witness doesn't need a law degree or technical training in jurisprudence. He simply takes the stand and tells the truth as he has known and experienced it. That's all that's required of us as Christ's witnesses. In our relational networks and in the opportunities God provides, we simply "take the stand," as it were, and bear testimony to the gospel as we've known and experienced it. We don't need to be brilliant, dynamic, or persuasive—we simply need to testify faithfully of what Jesus Christ has done to save sinners like us. Theological understanding and apologetic training, while helpful, are not prerequisites for this task, nor does their absence exempt us from responsibility. The only requirements are a saving knowledge of Christ and a willingness to obey our Lord by sharing his gospel.

Now, let me be the first to admit something: it's far easier to compose the paragraph I just typed than to apply it. No doubt most who read this paragraph *agree* with it. The question is, are we obeying? Am I alert to the opportunities afforded to me daily to speak for Christ—wisely, humbly, winsomely, yes; but to speak nonetheless? Am I ready to give an account for the hope I have in the gospel (1 Pet. 3:15)? Am I convinced that the gospel message itself—not my intellect or articulateness or wit—is "the power of God for salvation" (Rom. 1:16)? The response of others to the gospel lies outside our control. We have one responsibility: faithfulness to the privilege of bearing the gospel to people who desperately need it.

Thankfully, we don't bear this responsibility alone. The story of the Bible reminds us that God is not simply saving individuals but gaining a people for himself. And through the witness of this people, God's saving actions are put on display:

But you are a chosen race, a royal priesthood, a holy nation, a people for his own possession, that you may proclaim the excellencies of him who called you out of darkness into his marvelous light. (1 Pet. 2:9)

God holds up his church as Exhibit A for the reality of the gospel. As people called out of a fallen world, living transformed lives with transcendent values, the church displays the character of God, illustrates the power of God, and exemplifies the saving purposes of God. In fact, the church at *this* stage in salvation history has the privilege of signaling the *next* stage. Our life together gives the world a preview of life in the coming kingdom. George Ladd puts it this way:

> If Jesus' disciples are those who have received the life and fellowship of the Kingdom, and if this life is in fact an anticipation of the eschatological Kingdom, then it follows that one of the main tasks of the church is to display in this present evil age the life and fellowship of the Age to come. . . . [W]hile the church in this age will never attain perfection, it must nevertheless display the life of the perfect order, the eschatological Kingdom of God.[13]

Who dreamed that their church participation was so significant? Giving the world a glimpse of the consummated kingdom of God! Does such a grand vision govern our attitude toward our local churches? If it does, our participation will no doubt reflect it. We will love, serve, sacrifice, forgive, forbear, employ our gifts, mortify our pride—all that we might together "display in this present evil age the life and fellowship of the Age to come." Churches that display such a life, however imperfectly, are God's most potent instruments in his cosmic program to reclaim and restore his creation.

In Word and Deed

Strictly speaking, evangelism is sharing the message of the gospel, and the predicament of sinful people before a holy God invests this task with supreme urgency. However, the urgency of evangelism doesn't drain all other activity in this world of eternal significance. Once again, the Bible's story gives us perspective here: God remains committed to his creation, and he's actively working to restore it. As his redeemed image bearers, we have the privilege of laboring to see his dominion manifested throughout his creation. Swept into the kingdom of God, we now become agents of that kingdom in a fallen world.

Therefore, our daily lives in all their variety—vocation, relationships, study, community involvement, artistic endeavors, leisure—have the potential, when pursued for God's glory, to demonstrate something of the gospel and its effects. Every aspect of our involvement in this world is to have a redemptive component, illuminating the character of the Creator, imitating his activity, and embodying his intentions to save, renew, and restore. If we're appropriately "heavenly minded," we'll be alert to endless earthly opportunities to glorify God.

Take your job, for example. We should pursue our vocations in such a way that we model God's *redemptive intentions*. Different vocations will accomplish this differently, but all vocations can contribute to God's creation-restoring work. How can I serve others in my work? How can I display excellence? Model integrity? Alleviate suffering? More efficiently utilize God-given resources? Produce beauty? Seek justice? Our vocations are about far more than simply productivity and profit (although these should in no way be demeaned, reflecting as they do God's own fruitful activity). They provide untold opportunities to work for the extension of God's rule. Such activities follow naturally from the cosmic dimensions of Christ's rule, as John Murray reminds us: "There rests upon us . . . the obligation to bring to bear upon the whole compass of life the supernatural and redemptive forces that are inherent in the Christian redemption and revelation."[14]

Consider other spheres of your life. In my neighborhood or community, what avenues of involvement would enable me to "seek first the kingdom of God" (Matt. 6:33)? How might I serve the poor and underprivileged? How could I help to reverse inequities and establish justice? What gifts do I have that could be deployed for the good of my neighbors, the betterment of my community, the "welfare of [my] city" (Jer. 29:7)? Even though such activities may not directly communicate the gospel, they may well embody God's redemptive purposes by bringing peace and blessing to others.

Of course, such endeavors are not a substitute for the evangelistic task, although the distinction between these responsibilities is increasingly blurred in the evangelical world. Calls for mercy ministry, community transformation, and environmental concern, while legitimate and important, ring out with an urgency that often exceeds that attached to the evangelistic mandate. Unquestionably, Christians are to be salt and light in their communities (Matt. 5:13–14), working to see God's purposes extended in every possible way.

However, we must never forget what is at the core of God's redemptive activity: the salvation of people who bear his image and were created to know and glorify him. No other endeavor transcends this evangelistic priority. Our deeds may adorn the gospel message, but they must not be confused with the gospel message. Moreover, we should remain clear where our hope lies: only Christ's return will finally "redeem the culture," and our efforts to transform society, however legitimate, will always be partial. Like Abraham, we await a heavenly city (Heb. 11:8–16), which Christ will usher in at his return.

The World and the Cross

Enjoying the world, engaging the world, evangelizing the world—all are ways by which God calls us to be in the world and love the world. We receive God's earthly gifts, pursue God's purposes in earthly life, and work for the salvation of people made in God's image. All of life lived for the glory of God (1 Cor. 10:31).

Ah, but there's a tension. Isn't this a book about worldliness? Doesn't life in this world provide a myriad of temptations? Doesn't God's Word admonish, "Do not love the world"? How do we avoid worldliness while living a physical existence in a physical world that God created?

This book has sought to navigate between these two poles of the Christian life. It's not an easy journey. Most of us tend to gravitate toward one or the other of these aspects of our existence. The caricatures are easy to sketch.

Some have strictly spiritual preoccupations. For them, the present is of little consequence, pleasures are perilous, spirituality means self-denial. Their focus is on the fall, forgetting there's a good creation to be cared for and enjoyed.

Others relish life in this world. Their delight in God's temporal gifts is unrestrained, their enjoyment of their physical existence untempered, their hope in earthly endeavors absolute. Their focus is on the creation, forgetting there was a fall that brought sin and distortion to the world and to the human heart.

In navigating these polarities, a different moment in salvation history dominated the apostle Paul's horizon: "Far be it from me to boast except in the cross of our Lord Jesus Christ, by which the world has been crucified to me, and I to the world" (Gal. 6:14). For Paul, the cross was the singular, decisive, existence-altering reality of his life. No category of Paul's existence remained untouched by Christ's atoning death on his behalf.

The cross reinterpreted his past, revealing his sinfulness and the futility of his efforts to earn God's approval.

The cross also defined his present. Now, for Paul, "to live is Christ" (Phil. 1:21). Knowing Christ, pleasing Christ, serving Christ, glorifying Christ—Christ became the very meaning and purpose of Paul's life.

And, of course, the cross determined his future—if living is Christ, then "to die is gain" (1:21). All of Paul's hopes and joys lay in Christ, and death simply brought these to their fullest realization.

As a result, the cross was the crucial factor defining Paul's relationship with the world. On the one hand, the world was crucified to him. It held no sway over Paul, nor was he dependent upon it for anything. He didn't crave its approval, embrace its values, or covet its rewards. On the other hand, Paul had been crucified to the world. At his conversion, he was "crucified with Christ" (Gal. 2:20); in his union with Christ, his sins had been forgiven and his sinful nature crucified. Life in this world would never be the same.

How are you and I to view our existence in this world? Through the prism of Christ's saving work on the cross. The cross transforms all the categories of our lives. It answers the central questions of the human predicament.

The cross tells me who I am. Apart from grace, I'm a sinner separated from God and subject to his wrath, but through the cross I've been forgiven, adopted into God's family, and transformed by the Holy Spirit to know, love, and glorify God.

The cross interprets the world I inhabit. God made this world good, and although sin severely corrupted it, the cross demonstrates God's commitment to remove sin from his creation and his power to restore it to himself.

The cross transforms my view of people. Although made in the image of God, because of sin they are guilty, corrupt, and liable to punishment before a holy God. However, the gospel offers men and women hope, because on the cross Christ paid for the sins of all who would ever be forgiven.

The cross gives my life purpose. Through the cross I've been purchased by God and restored to his original purposes for me. I now can know him and glorify him in this world, reflecting his character and laboring to see his reign expressed throughout creation.

What part does the cross play in your life? Does it tower over all the other realities of your earthly existence? Does it define who you are and how you live? When we see our lives in light of what Jesus Christ accomplished on the cross, everything will be different. We won't be enamored of a fallen world that opposes God; it is for such a world that our Savior died. Nor will we ignore the world, untouched by its God-glorifying potential or unmoved by its needs. Rather, we'll take our place *in* this world, enjoying God's gifts, fulfilling God's purposes, and giving our lives to see the gospel proclaimed, sinners saved, and God glorified.

That's where the story—*God's* story—is heading. In ever-increasing ways, may we each take our place in this grand story and set our hope on its glorious conclusion.

Acknowledgments

Special thanks:

To Nicole Whitacre (my daughter): Big Girl, without your help I would not have been able to edit and write for this book. Without your help there would be no book! What a joy it was for me to work on this project with you. When you were a little girl you voiced your desire to write. I thought this was commendable, but I never thought you would be a published author. But God knew differently. God placed this desire to write in your heart so that one day you could serve your dad and mom with their writing projects. It moves me to tears as I think back to those days so many years ago when the Lord began to prepare you to serve your parents with your writing gift. And I'm sad this book has been completed, because I will miss talking about it with you each day. I love you with all my heart.

To Lane Dennis and Al Fisher for warmly welcoming a book on this topic and patiently enduring this writer throughout the process.

To Thomas Womack, Lydia Brownback, and Sarah Lewis, whose skillful editing made each chapter of this book clearer. We are grateful for their heart to humbly serve in the shadows.

To Sarah Lewis for the excellent discussion and application questions.

To Matt Wahl for his creative cover design.

To the many friends who helped us in some way with this book (and who might be looking for their names on this page). We are grateful for you. Were we to name everyone, the list would go on for pages! But while there are too many to thank individually here, we are aware of each one who helped, and we trust you feel our gratitude for your contribution to this book.

Appendix A

Modesty Heart Check

"WOMEN SHOULD ADORN themselves in respectable apparel, with modesty and self-control, not with braided hair and gold or pearls or costly attire, but with what is proper for women who profess godliness—with good works" (1 Tim. 2:9–10).

In his Word, God commands us to pursue the beauty of modesty and self-control both in our heart and in our dress. If we earnestly apply his Word to our hearts, it will be displayed by what we wear.

When it comes to selecting clothes to buy and wear, however, we can often feel lost and confused. Which items are seductive and immodest and which display a heart of modesty and self-control?

To assist you in cultivating a modest heart and maintaining a modest wardrobe, we humbly offer this Modesty Heart Check for your consideration.

We don't intend these questions to be a list of rules or consider them to be a definitive guide to modest dress. The Modesty Heart Check is a tool, to be used in the context of biblical teaching on modesty, and never in isolation from God's Word.

Appendix A

May these questions assist you as you seek to display the modest beauty of godly womanhood.

Carolyn Mahaney　　　　*Kristin Chesemore*

Nicole Whitacre　　　　*Janelle Bradshaw*

Start with a Heart Check

"How does a woman discern the sometimes fine line between proper dress and dressing to be the center of attention? The answer starts in the intent of the heart. A woman should examine her motives and goals for the way she dresses. Is her intent to show the grace and beauty of womanhood? . . . Is it to reveal a humble heart devoted to worshiping God? Or is it to call attention to herself, and flaunt her . . . beauty? Or worse, to attempt to allure men sexually? A woman who focuses on worshiping God will consider carefully how she is dressed, because her heart will dictate her wardrobe and appearance."[1]

• What statement do my clothes make about my heart?

• In choosing what clothes to wear today, whose attention do I desire and whose approval do I crave? Am I seeking to please God or impress others?

• Is what I wear consistent with biblical values of modesty, self-control, and respectable apparel, or does my dress reveal an inordinate identification and fascination with sinful cultural values?

• Who am I trying to identify with through my dress? Is my standard the Word of God or is it the latest fashion?

• Have I asked other godly individuals to evaluate my wardrobe?

• Does my clothing reveal an allegiance to the gospel, or is there any contradiction between my profession of faith and my practice of godliness?

Before you leave the house, do a modesty check. What are some things you should look for as you stand in front of your mirror?

From the Top

• When I am wearing a loose-fitting blouse or scoop neck, can I see anything when I lean over? If so, I need to remember to place my hand against my neckline when I bend down.

• Does this button-down top cause gaping holes that expose my chest? I need to turn sideways and move around to see. If there are revealing gaps, I've got to grab the sewing box and pin between the buttons.

• What about this sleeveless shirt? When I move around, can I see my bra? If I can, I need the pins again.

• Am I wearing a spaghetti-strap, halter, or sheer blouse? Not even pins will fix this problem! Most guys find these a hindrance in their struggle with lust. It's time to go back to the closet.

• Can I see the lace or seam of my bra through my shirt? In this case, seamless bras are a better option.

• Does my shirt reveal any part of my cleavage? Does my midriff show when I raise my hands above my head? Is my shirt just plain too tight? If the answer to any one of these questions is yes, then I need to change my outfit.

Moving on Down

• Does my midriff (or underwear) show when I bend over or lift my hands? If so, is it because my skirt or my pants are too low? Either my shirt needs to be longer or I need to find a skirt or pants that sit higher.

• Is what I'm wearing too tight around my backside, or does the outline of my underwear show? (You'll have to turn around to get a look here.) If so, I know what I have to do!

Appendix A

- Do these shorts reveal too much when I sit down? To see how much of my leg is exposed, I can't just check them standing up. If I see too much leg, I need a longer pair.
- Does this skirt or dress pass the sit-down check? I must remember to keep my skirt pulled down and my knees together when I'm seated.
- Does the slit in this skirt reveal too much when I walk? If so, pins are also helpful here.
- Does my skirt pass the sunlight check? Is it see-through? If so, I need a slip.
- What do these high heels do to the length of my skirt? I must remember to do this modesty check with my shoes on. Heels may make my dress or skirt appear shorter.

And don't forget—the modesty check applies to formal wear as well. A note on swimwear: It's not easy, but you can still strive to be modest at the pool or beach. Look for one-piece bathing suits that aren't cut high on the leg and don't have low necklines.

Appendix B

Considering Modesty on Your Wedding Day

(This document was originally created for use at Covenant Life Church in Gaithersburg, Maryland, and is reprinted here with permission.)

BEFORE YOU SET OUT on the exciting quest of finding that perfect wedding or bridesmaid dress, we want to encourage you to consider a question you'll be unlikely to hear any sales-lady ask you: "Will this dress selection bring glory to God?"

We know that your desire is to make your wedding day Godward in focus. God's Word in 1 Timothy 2:9–10 says, "Women should adorn themselves in respectable apparel, with modesty and self-control . . . with what is proper for women who profess godliness—with good works."

We as pastors desire to serve you in thinking about how you can apply God's Word, even to your wedding day.

First, please consider the purpose of your wedding day:

Albert Mohler reminds us, "What we are aiming for in the worship service of a wedding is to demonstrate the glory of

God in the coming together of a man and a woman in purity, in monogamy, and in faithfulness before Him; to be obedient to His commands and to receive all the goods and the gifts that are involved in the covenant of marriage."[1]

Second, please consider the following questions when shopping for a wedding or bridesmaid dress:

1) Does this dress reflect the fact that my wedding ceremony is a holy time of worship? (Our culture holds up this service as little more than a fashion show. You have an opportunity to draw attention to someone far more important than you: your Savior, Jesus Christ.)

2) Can I picture myself standing in this dress, for an extended period of time, just a few feet from my pastor as he opens the Bible and leads me in my solemn vows?[2]

3) Would I wear a dress (or other clothing) that is this revealing to a normal church service or on other days of the week?

Finally, here are some practical suggestions for choosing a wedding or bridesmaid dress:

1) Find a wedding dress with a neckline that conceals cleavage.

2) Look for dresses with sufficient covering in the back.

3) Be mindful that strapless gowns or dresses with only spaghetti straps are revealing and likely do not serve the men in attendance at your wedding.

If you are having trouble finding a modest dress in the bridal stores, consider having an affordable dressmaker make your dress. He or she may be able to create a dress for you based on pictures from a magazine or even ideas you give to him or her.

We hope these recommendations serve you in your effort to plan a ceremony that brings glory to God!

Discussion Questions

Chapter 1: Is This Verse in Your Bible?

For Your Mind

1) When the apostle John warns us, "Do not love the world or anything in the world" (1 John 2:15 NIV), what does he mean by "the world"?

2) Why is this warning relevant for every Christian?

3) How does 1 John 2:15–16 turn our focus away from externals to matters of the heart?

For Your Heart

4) Can you relate to any of these reasons for neglecting Scripture's command not to love the world?

- "Resisting worldliness" is just another way to say "out of touch."
- I can't evangelize the world if I don't relate to the world.
- No one has the right to tell me how much of the world I can take.
- My friends need this book more than I do.
- I'm not tempted to worldliness because I go to church—in fact, I attend Sunday meetings *and* a small group every week.
- If I think too seriously about it, I might have to let go of some things that I enjoy.

5) Is your Christian life marked by increasing love for the Savior? Or was there a time when you were consistently more passionate for God, and more characterized by extravagant devo-

tion and love for the church, than you are now? If the latter, why do you think this has happened?

6) What are you passionate about? What preoccupies you when your time and your thoughts are your own?

For Your Life

7) Is there something in the world you're presently attracted to or pursuing? It's probably whatever you've been thinking about as you read this chapter. If so, how can you seek accountability and help from a godly friend, parent, or pastor?

8) As this chapter points out, the antidote to worldliness is the cross of Jesus Christ. This is why Charles Spurgeon's counsel to "dwell where the cries of Calvary can be heard" is so valuable. What does Spurgeon mean by this? What is one way you can begin to follow his advice?

Chapter 2: God, My Heart, and Media

For Your Mind

1) Why is no one immune to the influence of media today?

2) As this chapter notes, hardly any discussion of media standards gets far before someone cries, "Legalism!" What is legalism? What is the only possible solution to legalism?

3) What does it mean to live *coram Deo*?

For Your Heart

4) How are you tempted to watch passively or with a sense of immunity as you surf the Internet or watch TV or films?

5) In what ways can you cultivate a greater awareness that every film, TV show, and Internet page you see is "before the face of God"?

6) Is your interest in keeping up with the latest TV shows and films hindering your growth in the Lord? If so, how? When you "need a break," what are you more likely to reach for—the remote? Fellowship with God and other believers? Something else?

For Your Life

7) This chapter explains that God-pleasing discernment involves remembering his grace to us in the death and resurrection of our Savior, and responding to his grace with a heart eager to please him by taking pleasure in what is good and right and true. How will this truth affect your decision about the next movie you watch?

8) If you limited your media choices to what was actually beneficial (as opposed to just permissible), would your viewing habits change? If so, how?

9) Does anyone know what you watch, how much you watch, and the specific areas in which you are tempted? If not, whom can you seek biblical accountability from?

Chapter 3: God, My Heart, and Music

For Your Mind

1) What indications do we have from the Bible that God likes music?

2) Why can't we create a list of artists or music styles that every Christian should listen to or avoid?

3) What do we mean when we say that music carries content, context, and culture?

For Your Heart

4) How important is music to you? Are you easily irritated when you aren't hearing the music you prefer? Are you more passionate about a concert than participation in your local church? More excited about the latest album than about the truth that Christ has saved you?

5) Does the music you listen to lead you to love the Savior more, or does it cause your affection for Christ to diminish?

6) Whose musical tastes are you most tempted to critique or look down on?

For Your Life

7) Do you own music that you'll listen to only if you backslide? If so, what reasons do you give for holding on to it?

8) As Harold Best points out, "There is no single chosen language or artistic or musical style that, better than all the others, can capture and repeat back the fullness of the glory of God." What is one thing you can do to broaden your musical taste?

9) Next Saturday night or Sunday morning, prepare for your church's Sunday meeting by taking time to thank the Lord for his gift of music and for those he's provided to lead your church in worship. What are some ways you can prepare your

heart and join in wholeheartedly when your church gathers for worship?

Chapter 4: God, My Heart, and Stuff

For Your Mind

1) *Covetousness* is a word we don't often use in normal conversation. What does it mean?

2) How is it that we can be covetous whether we're rich, poor, or anywhere in between?

3) How does the gospel specifically speak to the bondage of covetousness and materialism?

For Your Heart

4) Christ died to free you from loving stuff too much. What excites you about this truth? How should it influence our daily lives?

5) Describe a person you know who is regularly generous. How does that person reflect the eternal perspective of the gospel as he or she lets go of treasured possessions to benefit someone else? When was the last time God was so big for you that you let go of treasured possessions?

6) Are you giving regularly and generously to your local church? Describe why this is important to you, or why it is not your practice at present.

For Your Life

7) This chapter notes that when the gospel gets big, covetousness becomes weak. Reread John Owen's quote on page 108.

What does it mean to fill your affections with the cross and love of Christ?

8) This chapter points out that embracing covetousness can be a private sin, but casting it off should be a group project. Who will you enlist to help you cast off covetousness?

9) Parents, what steps can you take to train your children to share generously with others?

Chapter 5: God, My Heart, and Clothes

For Your Mind

1) Read 1 Timothy 2:3–10. What do these verses say about the motivation for modest dress?

2) How do we know that 1 Timothy 2:9 does not prohibit women from making themselves beautiful?

3) How do women who dress modestly serve men?

For Your Heart

4) Who are you trying to imitate or identify with through your appearance—godly women, or women of the world?

5) This chapter notes that your wardrobe is a public statement of your personal and private motivation. What does your clothing communicate about your motivations and priorities?

6) Think of a woman who is admired for her godly character and good works. What aspects of her godliness do you particularly want to imitate?

For Your Life

7) What about your wardrobe may need to change so that your appearance can better reflect the transforming power of the gospel?

8) What steps can you take on your next shopping trip to ensure that your clothing purchases reflect humility, modesty, and self-control? (Some ideas: Pray for God's help and provision in finding modest clothing; check each article of clothing you try on for modesty as well as fit; ask your father, husband, or a trusted friend to evaluate items you're not sure about.)

9) Mothers, what steps can you take to train your daughters to value godliness over fashion, to nurture humility and self-control, and to wear clothing that reflects these virtues? Fathers, what steps can you take to care for and lead your daughters in humility, self-control, and modesty?

Chapter 6: How to Love the World

For Your Mind

1) Can you relate to this chapter's description of "the Christian life by negation"? Do you think of the Christian life primarily in terms of what you're not supposed to do? How do John 3:16 and John 17:15–18 counteract this tendency?

2) If we think of the world's history as a story, what are the four main movements in the plotline, as this chapter presents them?

3) What three tasks enable us to "love the world" in a God-glorifying way?

For Your Heart

4) Read Galatians 6:14. Does Paul's perspective govern the way you view each area of your life (your identity, relationships, activities)? What difference should the gospel make in these areas?

5) Are you more excited about your own accomplishments, career, hobbies, or leisure time than about the glorious story of redemption? How might your perspective on these things change if you viewed them as part of *God's* program in the world?

6) This chapter notes that God holds up his church as Exhibit A for the reality of the gospel. Does this grand vision govern your attitude toward your own local church?

For Your Life

7) Think of one part of your work, education, leisure, or home life that seems insignificant or outside of God's notice. How does the truth that Christ is redeeming all of creation and restoring it to himself change the way you think about this area?

8) Are you actively involved and serving in your local church? If not, what practical steps can you take to contribute to your church's mission?

9) Think about the non-Christians you know. Do you take seriously the fact that they were made in the image of God? Do you also consider their *current* position before God, deserving of his eternal wrath? How might these twin realities motivate you to share the gospel with them?

Notes

Chapter 1: Is This Verse in Your Bible?

1. James Davison Hunter, *Evangelicalism: The Coming Generation* (Chicago: University of Chicago Press, 1987), 63.
2. Charles Spurgeon, "How to Become Fishers of Men" (sermon, Metropolitan Tabernacle, London, Sermon no. 1906; no date).
3. Charles Spurgeon, "Separating the Precious from the Vile" (sermon, Metropolitan Tabernacle, London, March 25, 1860).
4. Charles Spurgeon, "Confidence and Concern" (sermon, Metropolitan Tabernacle, London, August 8, 1886).
5. John Newton, "Glorious Things of Thee Are Spoken," hymn published 1779.
6. John Stott, *The Letters of John*, rev. ed. (Grand Rapids, MI: Eerdmans, 1988), 107.
7. Joel Beeke, *Overcoming the World: Grace to Win the Daily Battle* (Phillipsburg, NJ: P&R, 2005), 16 (emphasis mine).
8. Iain Murray, *Evangelicalism Divided: A Record of Crucial Change in the Years 1950 to 2000* (Carlisle, PA: Banner of Truth, 2000), 255.
9. David Jackman, *The Message of John's Letters* (Downers Grove, IL: InterVarsity, 1988), 61.
10. David Powlison, *Seeing with New Eyes: Counseling and the Human Condition through the Lens of Scripture* (Phillipsburg, NJ: P&R, 2003), 149.
11. John Calvin, *Institutes of the Christian Religion,* trans. Ford Lewis Battles, ed. John T. McNeil (Philadelphia: Westminster, 1960), 1:108.
12. John Owen, "Of Communion with God the Father, Son, and Holy Ghost," in *The Works of John Owen* (Johnstone and Hunter, 1850–1853; repr. Carlisle, PA: Banner of Truth, 1997), 2:150.
13. John Owen, *Sin and Temptation*, ed. and abr. James M. Houston (Vancouver: Regent, 1995), 62.
14. Charles Spurgeon, "To Lovers of Jesus" (sermon, Metropolitan Tabernacle, London, November 2, 1884).
15. Helen Howarth Lemmel, "Turn Your Eyes upon Jesus," hymn published 1922.

Chapter 2: God, My Heart, and Media

1. Dan Andriacco, *Taming the Media Monster* (Cincinnati, OH: St. Anthony Messenger Press, 2003), 5.
2. Kenneth A. Myers, *All God's Children and Blue Suede Shoes* (Wheaton, IL: Crossway Books, 1989), 160.
3. R. Kent Hughes, *Set Apart* (Wheaton, IL: Crossway Books, 2003), 51.

4. Myers, *All God's Children and Blue Suede Shoes,* xii–xiii.

5. C. J. Mahaney, *The Cross Centered Life* (Sisters, OR: Multnomah, 2002).

6. Wayne A. Wilson, *Worldly Amusements* (Enumclaw, WA: Winepress, 1999), 73.

7. Ibid., 64.

8. John Stott, *The Message of Ephesians* (Downers Grove, IL: InterVarsity, 1979), 193.

9. Philip Patterson, *Stay Tuned* (Webb City, MO: Covenant), 104.

10. Wilson, *Worldly Amusements*, 19.

Chapter 3: God, My Heart, and Music

1. Harold Best, *Music through the Eyes of Faith* (San Francisco: HarperCollins, 1993), 67.

2. Tim Wendel, in *USA Weekend* magazine, October 28, 2001.

3. Best, *Music through the Eyes of Faith*, 39–40.

4. In *Washington Post Magazine,* August 5, 2007, 20.

5. C. S. Lewis, "The Weight of Glory," in *The Weight of Glory and Other Addresses* (New York: MacMillan, 1980), 7.

Chapter 4: God, My Heart, and Stuff

1. Clearly, then, when Jesus speaks of himself as the "Son of Man," he is evoking an image that bears with it a story of conflict and kingship. It is no accident that Jesus' own gospel story is one of conflict with Satan and a proclamation of the presence and future fullness of the kingdom of God. The three contexts in the Gospels in which Jesus identifies himself by the image Son of Man—as one who seeks Israel's deliverance (e.g., Luke 19:10), who suffers Israel's exilic death and vindication (e.g., Mark 8:31; 10:45), and who is exalted and granted universal sovereignty (e.g., Mark 14:26)—all find their roots in Daniel's vision of "one like a son of man." It is a messianic image uniquely projected onto the gospel story and focused on the figure of Jesus.

2. Stuart Briscoe, "What Is Materialism," in *Inside the Sermon: Thirteen Preachers Discuss Their Methods of Preparing Sermons*, ed. Richard Allen Bodey (Grand Rapids, MI: Baker, 1990), 51.

3. April Witt, "Acquiring Minds: Inside America's All-consuming Passion," *The Washington Post Magazine* (December 14, 2003), 16.

4. *Illustrations for Biblical Preaching,* ed. Michael Green (Grand Rapids, MI: Baker, 1989), 179.

5. Gregg Easterbrook, *The Progress Paradox: How Life Gets Better While People Feel Worse* (New York: Random House, 2003), 161.

6. R. V. G. Tasker, "World," in *The New Bible Dictionary*, 2nd ed., ed. J. D. Douglas, et al. (Leicester, England: Inter-Varsity, 1982), 1261 (emphasis in original).

7. Randy Alcorn, *Money, Possessions and Eternity* (Wheaton, IL: Tyndale, 1989).

8. John Owen, *Sin and Temptation,* ed. and abr. James M. Houston (Vancouver: Regent, 1995), 62.

9. I. D. E. Thomas, quoting Thomas Brooks, *A Puritan Golden Treasury* (Carlisle, PA: Banner of Truth, 1977), 260.

10. Isaac Watts, *The Psalms of David Imitated in the Language of the New Testament* (London: J. Clark, 1719).

11. Alissa Quart, *Branded: The Buying and Selling of Teenagers* (Cambridge, MA: Perseus, 2003), xiii.

12. C. Samuel Storms, "Is Jesus *Really* Enough?" *Discipleship Journal*, no. 65 (1991): 62–63.

Chapter 5: God, My Heart, and Clothes

1. George W. Knight, *The Pastoral Epistles: A Commentary on the Greek Text*, New International Greek Testament Commentary (Grand Rapids, MI: Eerdmans, 1992), 133.

2. Abraham Kuyper, "Sphere Sovereignty," in *Abraham Kuyper: A Centennial Reader*, ed. James D. Bratt (Grand Rapids, MI: Eerdmans, 1988), 488.

3. John MacArthur, *1 Timothy*, The MacArthur New Testament Commentaries (Chicago: Moody, 1995), 80–81.

4. This paragraph and others in this chapter are taken with permission from the *Girl Talk* blog (http://www.girltalk.blogs.com) and were written by my wife, Carolyn, and my daughters, Nicole Whitacre, Kristin Chesemore, and Janelle Bradshaw.

5. This paragraph adapted from Carolyn Mahaney, "True Beauty," in *Biblical Womanhood in the Home*, ed. Nancy Leigh DeMoss (Wheaton, IL: Crossway Books, 2002), 41.

6. Carolyn Mahaney, "Fashion and Following the Savior, Pt. 4," http://girltalk.blogs.com/girltalk/2006/04/ fashion_and_fol_4.html.

7. John Angell James, *Female Piety* (Morgan, PA: Soli Deo Gloria, 1860; repr. 1995).

8. Carolyn Mahaney and Nicole Mahaney Whitacre, *Girl Talk: Mother-Daughter Conversations on Biblical Womanhood* (Wheaton, IL: Crossway Books, 2005), 141.

9. Nancy Leigh DeMoss, *The Look: Does God Really Care What I Wear?* (Buchanan, MI: Revive Our Hearts, 2003), 26.

10. Cited In Carolyn Mahaney, "Modesty on Your Wedding Day," http://girltalk.blogs.com/girltalk/2006/04/a_ pastors_plea.html (April 19, 2006).

11. Joan Jacobs Brumberg, *The Body Project* (New York: Random House, 1997), *xxi*.

12. Bryan Chapell, *1 and 2 Timothy and Titus: To Guard the Deposit,* Preaching the Word, ed. R. Kent Hughes (Wheaton, IL: Crossway, 2000), 63.

Chapter 6: How to Love the World

1. A wonderfully concise and accessible overview of a Christian worldview is found in Philip Graham Ryken's *What Is the Christian Worldview?* (Phillipsburg, NJ: P&R, 2006).

2. T. M. Moore, *Consider the Lilies* (Phillipsburg, NJ: P&R, 2005), 23.

3. John Calvin, *Institutes of the Christian Religion*, ed. John T. McNeill, trans. Ford Lewis Battles (Philadelphia: Westminster, 1960), 1.5.2; 52.

4. The term "general revelation" is used by theologians to designate God's revelation of himself through the natural creation and the human conscience.

It is "general" in the sense that it comes to all people equally, believer and non-believer alike.

5. For the derivation of "Eden," see Gordon Wenham, *Genesis 1–15,* Word Biblical Commentary, vol. 1 (Waco, TX: Word, 1987), 61.

6. Moore, *Consider the Lilies,* 26.

7. Abraham Kuyper, "Sphere Sovereignty," in *Abraham Kuyper: A Centennial Reader*, ed. James D. Bratt (Grand Rapids, MI: Eerdmans, 1988), 488.

8. Wayne Grudem, *God's Extraordinary Plan for Your Ordinary Days* (unpublished manuscript; quoted by permission), 42.

9. For a clear and concise introduction to a biblical view of vocation in all of life, and especially through work, see Gene Edward Veith Jr., *God at Work: Your Christian Vocation in All of Life* (Wheaton, IL: Crossway Books, 2002). Veith highlights Luther's emphasis on God working in and through our work.

10. For a clear and compelling treatment of the nature and task of evangelism, see Mark Dever's *The Gospel and Personal Evangelism* (Wheaton, IL: Crossway Books, 2007).

11. Grudem, *God's Extraordinary Plan,* 67.

12. Westminster Shorter Catechism, Question 1.

13. George Eldon Ladd, *A Theology of the New Testament*, rev. ed., (Grand Rapids, MI: Eerdmans, 1993), 113.

14. John Murray, "The Christian World Order," in *The Collected Writings of John Murray, Vol. 1: The Claims of Truth* (Carlisle, PA: Banner of Truth, 1976), 358.

Appendix A: Modesty Heart Check

1. John MacArthur, *1 Timothy*, The MacArthur New Testament Commentary (Chicago: Moody, 1995), 80–81 (emphasis added).

Appendix B: Considering Modesty on Your Wedding Day

1. Albert Mohler, *The Albert Mohler Radio Program*, May 16, 2006; available at http://www.albertmohler.com/radio_show.php?cdate=2006-05-16 (accessed April 2, 2008).

2. Questions 1 and 2 are adapted from remarks given by Todd Murray at The Bible Church of Little Rock, quoted by permission by Carolyn Mahaney in "Modesty on Your Wedding Day," http://girltalk.blogs.com/girltalk/2006/04/a_pastors_plea.html (accessed April 10, 2008).

.